When Living Hurts: For Teenagers, Young Adults, Their Parents, Leaders, and Counselors

By Sol Gordon, Ph.D.

When Living Hurts

A what-to-do book for yourself
or someone you care about who feels
discouraged, sad, lonely, hopeless,
angry or frustrated, unhappy,
bored, depressed, suicidal

Third Edition

Sol Gordon, Ph.D.

URJ Press· New York, New York

Dedication

To my "prodigal" son Josh who has "come home" at last!

And to my friend Rabbi Dan Syme, whose ideas and support inspired my book in the first place.

Sol Gordon

The author gratefully acknowledges permission by Ric Masten to use his poem "Hands."

Library of Congress Cataloging-in-Publication Data

Gordon, Sol, 1923-
When living hurts : for teenagers, young adults,
their parents, leaders, and counselors /
by Sol Gordon.– Rev. ed.
        p. cm.
Includes bibliographical references.
ISBN 0-8074-0864-6 (pbk. : alk. paper)
1. Youth–Suicidal behavior. 2. Suicide–Prevention.
3. Adolescent psychology. I. Title.
HV6546.G67 2003
362.28'0835–dc22

2004005116

Contents

INTRODUCTION   1

FRAGMENTS OF AN AUTOBIOGRAPHY   3

**1   WHAT TO DO IF YOU OR A FRIEND
NEEDS HELP   5**

Do you have a good reason to feel bad?   5

Are you feeling sad, unhappy, depressed?   6

Are you lonely?   11

Seven messages   14

What's a mensch?   15

Mitzvah therapy   17

Hooked on drugs or alcohol?   18

*Eight key messages about drug and
alcohol abuse*   21

If you don't like the way you look   22

Are you bored or are you boring?   24

How to overcome boredom   26

*Do you have a disability or do you know
someone who does?*   28

Contents

You can't please everybody!   30

Are you very angry?   31

Are you being teased, bullied, or left out?   32

Do you feel empty inside?   33

Meditation   37

Did something terrible happen to you when
you were a child?   38

Living well is the best revenge   39

What was the worst thing that ever happened to you?
40

Do most people fall short of your expectations?
41

Do you have disturbing thoughts?   42

Friendship   44

2 IF YOU OR SOMEONE YOU KNOW IS SUICIDAL   47

How to get help urgently   47

How to help someone who is in a panic or
having what's sometimes called an anxiety attack
50

Dying to live the good life?   52

What to do if someone you care about
is suicidal   55

Contents

Do not keep a suicidal intent confidential   60

Can you tell the difference between a cry for help, a wish for attention, and depression?   62

Possible suicide warning signs   65

Why are so many young people killing themselves?   66

What if you think that life isn't worth living?   67

Why teens commit suicide   68

A letter from a bereaved mother   73

Suggestions for survivors by Iris Bolton   76

3 SEX AND LOVE: WORRIES AND FACTS   79

Are you worried about sex?   79

AIDS alert and STD (sexually transmitted disease) cautions   81

Sexual fantasies   85

Masturbation   86

Homosexuality   88

More on sexual orientation   95

Pregnancy   97

Virgin rights   98

Contents

How can you tell if you are really in love?   99

Dying for love   102

4   PARENT CONCERNS   105

If you don't get along with your parents   105

A message to you: don't turn off your parents   107

Did a divorce or separation—or living with a stepparent—mess you up?   110

A message to parents   112

"Askable" parents raise sexually responsible children   120

5   GOD CONCERNS   125

Are you disappointed in God?   125

Have you lost faith in religion?   126

Do you feel in need of prayer?   127

6   WHAT IS THE PURPOSE OF LIFE?   129

Does life have a purpose?   129

How does forgiveness work?   132

If you can't forgive someone who hurt you or if you can't accept the idea of forgiveness   133

It's never too late   134

Contents

When someone you love has died   135

How is hope renewed?   136

7   **IDEAS TO PUSH YOU INTO THINKING ABOUT YOUR LIFE   137**

Eighteen slogans and thoughts   140

Thoughts and things to do for the next eighteen days 142

Think about it!   143

8   **A SPECIAL MESSAGE FOR SCHOOL COUNSELORS AND YOUTH LEADERS   151**

Why "at-risk" youth do not pay attention to what we (so-called) educators have to say   151

9   **APPENDIX: CHOICE USA: LEADERSHIP FOR A PRO-CHOICE FUTURE   159**

The difference between Emergency Contraception and Mifepristone (RU-486)   159

10   **RESOURCES   163**

I write for people of all faiths, little faith, no faith, and especially for those still searching. I encourage you to stand for something.

Otherwise you may fall for anything.

Sol Gordon

x

Believe that life is worth living and your belief will help to create the fact.
—William James

The secret of wisdom is kindness.
—Charles B. Haywood

Advice from a teenager who has attempted suicide: No matter how bad things may seem, they will get better. Just hold on.

Nobody is weirder than anyone else—some people just take longer to understand.
—Tom Robbins, *Even Cowgirls Get the Blues*

Be grateful for luck. Pay the thunder no mind— listen to the birds. And don't hate nobody.
—Eubie Blake

The great Jewish sage Hillel reminds us: "If I am not for myself, who will be for me? If I am only for myself, what am I? And if not now, when?"

What do you think Hillel says to us now?

There is an ever-present need to enhance ourselves, and our spiritual aspirations, but we must never forget our obligations to society lest we discover one day that it is too late.

The world is full of people who in the guise of piety
are ready to harness others.
—Baal Shem Tov

Repeat over and over again, "I shall either find a
way or make one." Or, in Latin, if you prefer, *"Aut
inveniam viam aut faciam."*

And then say, "I will be gentle with myself, I will
love myself, I am part of the universe."
—Joseph and Nathan

Introduction

This is a book for people who want to help others who are in trouble.

It is also for people who are lonely, depressed, or suicidal.

My basic message is that we are all our brothers' and sisters' keepers, and that living well is the best antidote for hopelessness, helplessness, feeling unloved, unfairness, and tragedy. This book focuses on how to cope with disappointments and imperfections (in an imperfect world).

There are a lot of things people say to try to make you feel better. But they don't really help, and sometimes they might even make you feel worse.

- Don't worry. (When's the last time someone told you not to worry and you stopped?)

- Don't feel guilty. (If you've done something wrong, maybe you should feel guilty.)

- You can be anything you want to be. (You should live so long.)

- Get rid of unrealistic expectations. (How do you know in advance that your expectations are unrealistic?)

- If you eliminate shoulds, musts, perfectionist tendencies, worries, and other imperfections, you'll be happy. (So what else is new?)

The plain fact is that life, in large part, is made up of things to worry about—not only personal things but the state of the world, including hunger, racism,

Introduction

terrorism, crime-infested cities, disasters, personal tragedies, and despair.

Life can be unfair, unlucky, uninteresting, and unnerving for large parts of the day or even for years at a time.

Real people have bad moods, experience periods of depression, and fall in love with people who don't love them.

Life can also be full of joys, pleasures, and excitement. These sensations may not last long, but they are nevertheless real.

I don't want you to pretend. But you can change the impact of reality by changing how you feel about it. You can acknowledge the pain of your real world, and by being helpful to others, by reaching out beyond your own pain, you can renew and revitalize yourself.

This book is also about promoting self-esteem. I like the definiton of self-esteem developed by the California Legislative Task Force on Self-Esteem (1990): "Appreciating my own worth and importance and having the character to be accountable for myself and to act responsibly toward others."

Caution: Don't fall for the trap of equating self-esteem with "feeling good about yourself," which can sometimes result in selfish, greedy, and uncaring behavior. It is surprising how many people "feel good" about themselves while putting down those around them.

Fragments of an Autobiography

Sometimes one finds oneself in a grim situation. There is nothing one can do about it except to wait for a brighter future. I remember my own childhood as a sad and lonely time. I hated school and often was in conflict with my parents. I contemplated suicide and imagined that everybody would be sorry. It was hard to avoid thinking about irrational ways out of my situation.

I began to feel better in my late teen years when I realized that there is nothing wrong with being unhappy every once in a while. There are times when being unhappy or profoundly sad is the appropriate response, especially when someone you love dies or betrays you.

It is not always easy to tell when unhappiness is based on irrational thoughts or guilt feelings. Irrational unhappiness comes equipped with symptoms like depression, alcohol or drug abuse, pains without actual disease, feelings of anxiety, despair and emptiness, an inability to feel motivated, a gross loss of appetite, overeating, sexual compulsions, and/or a tendency to be mean and abusive.

Rational sadness is mostly grand, dignified, private, a bit heroic, unselfish, free of irrational guilt or pride. It ends up being a learning experience, however much a person may have suffered. For example: When you break up with your girlfriend or boyfriend, you are in pain. But you can choose to make every effort not to cause pain to others as well. You can use this time to reexamine your goals in life.

Keep in mind that it is difficult to think yourself into correct acting. You need to act yourself into correct thinking.

Chapter 1

What to Do if You or a Friend Needs Help

Lesley Hazleton writes:

To be fully alive means to experience the full range of emotions, to struggle with the downs as well as to enjoy the ups. Life is certainly difficult and even unpredictable— full of meaning and purpose at one time and utterly meaningless and purposeless at another, sometimes so desirable that we wish to freeze it at a certain point and remain there forever, and at other times so undesirable that we may find ourselves wishing we had never been born. But it also has its own dynamics. There is no real happiness without the experiences of depression to balance it. If we are not capable of depression, we are not capable of happiness either. In a very real sense, depression keeps us alive.

—*The Right to Feel Bad—Coming to Terms with Normal Depression* (Dial Press, 1984)

Do you have a good reason to feel bad?

"Nothing in life just happens. It isn't enough to believe in something. You have to have stamina to meet obstacles and overcome them, to struggle...." —Golda Meir

5

Are you feeling sad, unhappy, depressed?

Almost everyone feels bad, down, or miserable occasionally. Ordinary depression strikes everyone from time to time. But some of us suffer from it more often than others. In this book, when we use the word *depression*, we mean sadness, despair, unhappiness. These feelings can be appropriate when tragic events occur but they are not the same as the term *clinical depression*, which is considered a mental illness. Clinical depression is rarely found or diagnosed among young people before the age of twenty. The cause of clinical depression is in dispute and its origin is not known.

This book is not concerned with temporary upsets, such as an event that was spoiled by the weather, or someone's bad mood. Such feelings are responses to real situations and usually don't last long or cause symptoms like fears and physical problems. When we use the word *depression* here we merely refer to a response to irrational ideas such as blaming yourself for something that you were not responsible for—all those "should've," could've," "would've" situations in your life. Depression often occurs because, for one reason or another, you feel inferior. Perhaps you relentlessly compare yourself unfavorably to others.

There will always be people who are luckier, richer, better looking, or smarter than you are. Even so, each person is unique. No one in the world is exactly like you. Could it be that we are all on earth for a special mission or purpose? As Eleanor Roosevelt once said, "No one can make you feel inferior without your consent."

It's important to deal with depression as early as possible because it can lead to serious problems, such as headaches, fears, obsessions, nightmares, insomnia, or a chronic state of feeling hopeless and inferior.

Many people deal with feelings of unhappiness in a self-destructive way. They eat too much or too little. Or they drink alcohol or take drugs to numb their feelings. Alcohol and drugs might make you feel good for a while, but then you usually feel worse than before. You have a hangover and you feel sick, terrible, alone, and miserable.

What should you do if you're feeling depressed?

THERE IS HARDLY ANYTHING

MORE ENERGIZING

THAN LEARNING SOMETHING NEW.

IT'S THE FIRST STEP IN

GETTING OUT OF A DEPRESSION.

Here are some suggestions to get you started:

- Send an e-mail or snail mail to someone who would be surprised to hear from you.

- Go to a park, museum, play, or somewhere you rarely think of going.

- Watch a program on television that you wouldn't ordinarily watch, like a PBS documentary or a nature show.

- Go see a serious movie.

- Don't watch TV for a whole day. (Better yet, don't watch TV for a whole week.) Find out what radio has to offer aside from you favorite music.

7

- Get into a new sport.
- Write down all the things you like to do. Then without giving the matter much thought, do one of the things on your list.
- Daydream without feeling guilty.
- Fix or build something.
- Volunteer your services for a good cause.
- Write a poem.
- Buy a magazine you wouldn't ever imagine yourself reading. Consider *The New Yorker*, *Rolling Stone*, or *Psychology Today*, and read at least two articles in it.
- Get a dog, cat, or some tropical fish.
- Grow some plants.
- Make a decision to collect something (stamps, coins, cactus plants).
- If nothing else works, try exercise.

This list is a start. In the long run, there is no substitute for feeling secure about yourself. This happens mainly when you have a sense of purpose or a mission in your life—a feeling that life is worthwhile because your life is meaningful!

IF YOU ARE INTERESTED,

PEOPLE WILL BE INTERESTED IN YOU.

If you don't feel that your situation is urgent or a crisis, try reading *Do One Thing Different: Ten Simple Ways to Change Your Life* by Bill O'Hanlon (Quill, 2000).

You'll start feeling better when you put a little effort into learning something new; when you feel good about doing something for someone else; when you begin to plan ahead instead of worrying ahead; and most of all when you stop comparing yourself to other people.

If you've been depressed a long time and are not sure why, schedule a complete medical examination. Something may be physically wrong with you that is affecting your mental state. Medication might help, but only temporarily. Get into therapy or seek counseling with a person you trust. You may find that you are more able to confide in a professional than in someone you know. Professionals are trained to listen and be helpful. We can't always say that about friends. A warning: Don't stay with a therapist whom you don't like. Think twice about continuing to see someone if you haven't experienced a significant improvement after about ten sessions. For most people, some improvement is evident early in the treatment. In addition, read carefully the sections of this book that are pertinent to you.

If you have a friend who is depressed, you are probably concerned about how that person is managing when you are not around. You may want to keep tabs on your friend without making it seem that you are invading his or her privacy. Try to be supportive and available to talk about your friend's situation and feelings. When you leave his or her company, be sure you say something that lets your friend know you are still with him or her in spirit. To convey your availability, say something like:

9

- Call me if you want to talk or get together.

- I can't know how you actually feel, but I know it's tough for you right now. I hope you will share your feelings with me.

- I'm your friend. I care for you.

Whatever words you use, be sure your friend knows that you care and are ready to help.

The most painful kind of loneliness is the loneliness that makes you feel hopeless and desperate.

Strangely enough, the loneliest people often feel most unhappy when they are among others, even in crowds.

Loneliness is a state of mind. Lots of people enjoy being alone sometimes. They even savor the precious moments when they are alone, using the time to read, reflect, or just relax. It is their choice.

It is a different matter if you are alone without wanting to be. But even when you are alone, you can put being alone to good use. There are lots of things you can do when you are by yourself.

Are you lonely?

- Read.

- Keep a daily journal.

- Listen to you favorite music.

- Eat and dress well.

- Treat yourself to a leisurely bath.

- Clean your room (apartment).

- And you know what? It's okay to talk to yourself. (You can figure out a lot of things that way.)

- Call a cousin whose company you enjoy and plan on getting together.

- Look over the family album.

- Rent a movie.

- Go for a long walk.

- What about a hobby? One you've been thinking about for a long time.

Although it is hard to think about reaching out to others when we feel lonely, changing our focus can really help. But it does take some motivation.

11

For some people, loneliness lasts a long time. I was lonely most of my childhood. I wasn't good at athletics. Kids made fun of me because I was a redhead. I was clumsy. I survived by daydreaming and reading books. In my late teens I went to libraries and museums where I talked to people. It was in a museum that I met one of my best friends. As my life improved at home and school, I started to see things differently. Exactly how it happened I am not sure. I only know that life became good once more.

Here is a list of a few books I have found to be pleasurable and insightful:

- *Living a Life that Matters* by Harold Kushner (Knopf, 2001)

- *The Art of Happiness* by the Dalai Lama and Howard C. Cutler (Riverhead Books, 1998)

- *Man's Search for Meaning* by Victor E. Frankl (Beacon Press, 2000)

- *The Road Less Traveled* by M. Scott Peck (Simon and Schuster, 1978)

- *The Way of Man* by Martin Buber (reissue ed., Lyle Stuart Hardcover, 1995)

- *Thoughts Without a Thinker* by Mark Epstein (Basic Books, 1995)

- *For Those Who Can't Believe: Overcoming the Obstacles to Faith* by Harold M. Schulweis (Harper Collins, 1994)

Novels and autobiographies that deal with the purpose of life include:

- *The Color Purple* by Alice Walker (10th anniv. ed., Harcourt, 1992)

- *The Snow Leopard* by Peter Matthiessen (Viking, 1978)
- *The Book of Laughter and Forgetting* by Milan Kundera (Alfred A. Knopf, 1980)
- *Siddhartha* by Herman Hesse (New Directions Publishing, 1951)
- *Wake Up, I'm Fat* by Camryn Manheim (Broadway Books, 1999)
- *The Painted Bird* by Jerzy Kosinski (2d ed., Random House, 1983)
- *The Diary of a Young Girl* by Anne Frank (1947)

I also recommend novels by Tim O'Brien, Russell Banks, E. L. Doctorow, Kurt Vonnegut, Herman Melville, Irvin Yalom, Anne Tyler, Cynthia Ozick, John Steinbeck, Sholem Asch, Albert Camus, Franz Kafka, Erica Jong, Andre Gide, Thomas Mann, John Dos Passos, Iris Murdoch, Saul Bellow, Virginia Woolf, Amos Oz, I. B. Singer, Ernest Hemingway, Elie Wiesel, Owen Dodson, James Baldwin, Thomas Wolfe, Romain Rolland, Phillip Roth, Leon Uris, and James Michener.

Russell Baker's autobiography *Growing Up* (Congdon and Weed, 1982) is inspirational, as is Eudora Welty's *One Writer's Beginnings* (Harvard Univ. Press, 1984). Paul Cowan's *An Orphan in History* (Doubleday, 1982) probably would interest anyone concerned about his or her Jewish identity.

If you are not into reading, that's okay. You could move into fitness and exercise to build your body. Or you might try meditation or yoga. You could even find out more about your religion.

Seven Messages

- Take emotional and intellectual risks. Unless you are willing to risk being rejected, you will never know the joy of feeling accepted.

- Try to do the right thing for yourself. You can't live trying to measure up to other people's expectations.

- If you feel attractive, you'll attract people. If you feel unattractive, you'll give off bad vibrations.

- Loneliness is a temporary state. Use the time to be nice to yourself. Don't be mean to your family. If you are lonely, it may not be somebody else's fault.

- A person who fails at something is not a failure. Failure is an event, not a person.

- "A person will be called to account on judgment day for every permissible thing that he or she might have enjoyed but did not." (Jerusalem Talmud)

- "One person of integrity can make a difference." (Elie Wiesel)

14

Without aspiring to be a mensch,
being alive is a burden.

We all start out human.
No way can we be more so
or less so.

We are at all times
struggling with the good and the bad
parts of ourselves.

Our free will represents the heart
of becoming a mensch.

A mensch is someone who
aspires to be
a good person
and is,
most of the time.

A good person is
someone who accepts the biblical injunction to
Love Thy Neighbor As Thyself.

This is not easy, especially for those
who don't love themselves.
The best way to change
is by being nice to others;
then you may at least
feel good about yourself.

If you bless others,
you can then bless yourself.
If you can afford to see good in others,
you'll come to see good in yourself.

But there is still a catch.
Not everyone is in harmony
with your timing.

What's a mensch?

15

Not everyone is receptive
to your kindess.

A really important obligation
of a mensch is to do
mitzvot, "good deeds."

A person does mitzvot without expecting
something in return.
But mitzvot always bring you rewards.

A mensch is a good person
who has faith in humanity
and expresses it with a selfless love.

My mother (of blessed memory)
used to say to us in Yiddish,
Zut a gut vort. Est cost nit mare.
"Say a good word. It doesn't cost more."
She was a mensch.
My life is a struggle to become one.
The hardest part of becoming a mensch
is forgiveness.

I have been a psychotherapist and counselor most of my professional life, but in recent years I've found that in many cases I could be even more helpful by proposing mitzvah therapy, often as an alternative (sometimes as an addition) to counseling.

One very bright young woman, revealed to me after five years of psychoanalysis, that she was more miserable than ever. She had been abused as a child, had no friends, was suicidal and depressed, and she begged me for help.

Mitzvah therapy

I proposed that she volunteer at an institution for abused children. After one month of volunteering almost daily, she reported that she had never felt happier in her whole life. For the first time she felt needed, wanted, and appreciated. The children at the institution adored her, and she realized that she didn't have to start out by loving herself in order to be helpful and loving to others in need.

A suicidal high school student who was constantly bullied was not helped much after years of counseling. He was transformed after I encouraged a high school football star to protect and mentor him.

A detention center for juvenile delinquents "turned around" most of the inmates after they spent a year working with seriously handicapped high school students.* Again, for the first time in their lives, these delinquents felt needed, wanted, and appreciated.

---

* In follow-up studies, the recidivism (reconviction) rate was less than 25 percent, as compared to previous figures of 80 percent.

No matter what your problem is, you can't solve it with alcohol or drugs. Even if you are able to continue functioning while using alcohol or drugs, you'll become less productive, as well as nasty to people who care about you. You'll spoil any chances you might have had for an intimate relationship.

People who are hooked characteristically:

Hooked on drugs or alcohol?

- Lie a lot.

- Can't be trusted (because they frequently make and break promises).

- Are overconfident (and tend to say things like, "Don't worry, I can handle it").

- Give priority to the addiction (over everything else in their lives, including intimate relationships).

- Have poor judgment (which makes it difficult for them to drive, among other things).

- Become irrational and volatile, and even violent.

If you can't stop drinking or using drugs on your own (or if your friend can't), a crisis intervention clinic will tell you where you can get help. Once you are addicted or a chronic user of any drug, it's difficult to stop without professional support. Getting help is an act of courage. Not getting help leads to despair and hurting the people you care about the most.

Here is something else you need to know. Just getting off the stuff will not automatically solve your problems. You will still need time, patience, energy, and motivation to make new friends and develop new interests. The most difficult period is the first three or four weeks after stopping. This is a period of high anxiety and tension. It's the time to learn something new, find a hobby, try a new sport, exercise a lot, or get involved helping others who are in worse shape than you are. Above all, don't expect to be perfect and don't expect anyone to appreciate what you are trying to accomplish. It is a gift you are giving to yourself.

Learning to cope with this transitional period of anxiety is just as important as stopping substance abuse. Otherwise you might start again. But even if you do start again (and many do), you need to keep in mind that you can always stop again.

The main thing is to get help *right away*. A group such as Alcoholics Anonymous is a good place to start. If you are not into a spiritually oriented approach, try an alternative recovery group. Start by reading *Sober for Good* by Anne M. Fletcher (Houghton Mifflin, 2001). Finding a sponsor or partner who can help you stay sober is also important.

If you are troubled by someone else's drinking, Al-Anon/Alateen can help. Call 1-888-AL-ANON (425-2666).

Someone I know well wrote this:

> Overcoming any addiction hinges on the ability to acquire a shift in perception.

> Addicts run from difficult emotions and cling for their lives to enticing ones.

Then he encouraged all addicts to take this serenity prayer seriously:

19

God grant me the serenity
To accept the things I cannot change,
Courage to the change the things I can,
and wisdom to know the difference.

Read *Hour to Hour: The First Thirty Days* [of recovery for the chemically dependent] by Shelly Marshall, P. O. Box 216, Ruthville, VA 23147.

Another suggestion is *Young, Sober and Free: Experience, Strength, and Hope for Young Adults* by Shelly Marshall.

- Don't drive under the influence!

- If someone says, "I'm not drunk. I can drive!" he or she is probably drunk and shouldn't drive.

- If one or both of your parents are alcoholics, you may have a predisposition to alcoholism.

- Alcohol, illegal drugs, and legal drugs (such as cigarettes) are all poison to the unborn. They can lead to a variety of birth defects that drastically affect the entire life of a baby.

- One small mistake, like driving while drunk, can take or seriously impair your life and the lives of innocent people.

- One or two drinks, as Shakespeare wrote, "provoke the desire," but more than that will "take away the performance." Impotence (the inability to maintain an erection) often occurs if a man drinks too much and then tries to have sex.

- People in the chronic stages of alcoholism begin to act like their own worst enemy and seriously damage their health, resulting in premature death.

- People "under the influence" are more likely to engage in unprotected sex, which can lead to pregnancy, sexually transmitted diseases, and HIV/AIDS.

Please note: Until addicts start to deteriorate from the effects of drugs they often appear to be nice, lively, interesting people. That's why it's easy for them to fool almost everybody. What they need is help.

Eight key messages about drug and alcohol abuse

21

If you don't like the way you look

We all have the "Perfect Body" image in our heads. It was put there by magazines, movies, and television bombarding us with the messages that being thin for girls and muscular for boys will guarantee success and fulfillment. Anything that deviates from that image we view in an exaggerated way—whether it is our nose, thighs, arms, or total body weight. The current ideal image is reinforced by diet and fitness programs that promise sure and quick results but which mostly do not work.

If you are overweight, try to change your diet by cutting down on foods high in sugar and starches, like non-diet sodas, and French fries. But starving yourself is not a solution, and is very dangerous. It is essential to eat a high volume of fruits, vegetables, and whole grains in their most natural and fresh state. Following these simple rules, combined with regular exercise, will bring your weight down and keep it that way.

Most people overeat because they are anxious. Learn to find the emotional triggers that make you revert to overeating. Find alternative ways to reduce tension, such as a hobby, a sport activity like biking, swimming, or jogging, or try yoga or meditation.

The truth is that even if you lose weight, you still have to work on your self-esteem. You can change certain aspects of your appearance, but you must also change your attitude about how you look. People who accept themselves are attractive to other people. It is not true that only people who are conventionally attractive find mates, but it is true that people who hate themselves tend to repel rather than attract others.

Exercise, especially in groups, can be most enjoyable as well as beneficial. Learn a sport, learn to dance, join a team, and work on a skill you can take pride in.

Misleading information, often related by hearsay or fads, can lead to worries about certain parts of the body. Men may worry about the size of their penises. Actually, the size of a penis is unrelated to sexual gratification. Women are concerned about the size of their breasts. The popularity of small or large breasts seems to change with fashion. Again, breast size has little to do with sexual pleasure, and when men outgrow their "locker-room mentality" about breasts, they are able to view women as people and not as objects of adolescent fantasy.

You can easily blame your appearance or some imagined physical "defects" for any problem you have, but that would be a cop-out. Why not focus instead on your personality, your generosity, your curiosity for learning and expanding your mind, and all the good qualities you possess that are not related to your looks?

THERE IS SOMEBODY FOR EVERYBODY

WHO FEELS REASONABLY GOOD

ABOUT HIMSELF OR HERSELF.

Everyone is bored now and then. That's of no particular significance. It's only when boredom becomes a way of life that you have to do something. There is nothing more uninteresting than a bunch of people standing around talking about how bored they are.

Are you bored or are you boring?

Here is a list of the most boring things you can do:

· Put yourself down. Tell yourself and others how worthless and rotten you are.

· Tell friends who ask how you feel about your bad points.

· Tell people you're horny.

· Boast about things that everybody knows you haven't done.

· Watch TV a lot. Have you noticed that the more you watch TV, the more bored you get?

· Constantly talk about only one subject (sports, sex, movies). It's okay if you have one main interest, but if that's all you talk about, people will tune out.

· Always come across as a Pollyanna ("Oh, everything is wonderful!") or as a cynic ("Life stinks!").

· Relentlessly tell people how tired you are.

· Talk too much. You are not as boring if you talk too little, as long as you participate by listening.

· Be absolute about everything.

· Complain a lot.

24

- Be paranoid and suspicious about everyone's motives.

- Be overdependent on what other people think.

- Approach people by saying, "I don't want to trouble you, bore you, or take up too much of your time." That's fake humility.

- Be unwilling to try new experiences.

- Be a supermiser. You don't want to do interesting things because you "can't afford it." You don't know if you will ever be able to afford it.

- Persistently analyze other people's behavior and motives.

- Gossip.

- Nearly always wait to be asked and hardly ever do the asking.

- Be serious and humorless most of the time, or always kid around.

- Relieve your tension by using drugs or alcohol.

- Spoil other people's stories (because you've said, thought, or heard them before).

- Announce how self-sacrificing you are and what ungrateful slobs the other people around you are.

- Complain that there's nothing to do, or talk endlessly of plans for the future that usually don't pan out.

- Always insist on being the center of attention.

25

How to overcome boredom

Being bored is very tiring. It's no accident that when employers want something done, they ask their busiest employee to do it. The more you do, the more alert you are and the more time you have to do all the things you want to do.

When you are bored, you also need to be especially careful about not taunting, tormenting, or hurting other people. Boredom is often one of the major causes of senseless delinquent acts and other evils.

The best medicine for overcoming boredom is to do or learn something new or different. This will give you a first-class rush, which can then motivate you to do or learn more.

You'll also become alert, energized, stimulated, and more confident. Now is the time to do things. It doesn't matter whether it's cleaning house, getting a ball game started, baking a cake, doing all the odd jobs you've been putting off, or finally starting a big project that you've been dreaming about.

While pulling yourself out of a bored state may seem difficult, if you are willing to take a chance and follow the suggestions listed below, you may not find it as hard as you originally thought it would be.

When you eat or drink something with sugar in it, you'll feel better instantly, but the physical effect will last only for about two minutes. Then you probably will want to eat more, and if you do, you might end up feeling worse than when you started. So here's the trick: Once you have eaten something sweet, begin doing something new or different right away. You have two minutes to start.

Here are some ideas:

- Read an article that will give you some new information.

- Renew a friendship that you've neglected. Risk its working or not working out.

- Let someone close to you know that you are in a good mood.

- Take a fast walk for twenty minutes. Look at the scenery, and if you are alone, make up a story about what you see.

- Do an art project. Make a birthday card for someone close to you. Make a collage. Paint an old chair in fun colors. Make a mobile for your room.

- Offer to weed or mow the yard of a neighbor or relative. (Of course, your own home might need some help.)

- Ask someone over for a lunch you have made, or make a dessert for your family.

- Sign up for a course.

- Volunteer to help those who are less fortunate.

- Visit an elderly relative.

27

If you yourself do not have a disability, you probably know someone who does. According to the American Coalition of Citizens with Disabilities, about 36 million Americans today—roughly one in six—suffer serious physical, mental, or emotional impairment.

Having a disability might create all kinds of difficulties—social, emotional, sexual, and economic. Part of the problem is that people with disabilities are often excluded from the mainstream of life by the rest of us.

Do you have a disability or do you know someone who does?

As a psychologist who has worked with people with disabilities, I offer the following advice to people who are not "impaired": Make an effort to befriend a person with disabilities. Do it with empathy and compassion. Form your friendship on the basis of a common interest or by helping the person develop an interest in something that you already enjoy. Once you have established a relationship, don't treat your friend with exaggerated delicacy or sensitivity. In particular, don't hesitate to communicate your feelings. For example, you may find that your friend is misinterpreting your interest as love. If this is the case, the sooner you clear up the misunderstanding the better.

The following is another important point: It's all right if you start out feeling uncomfortable. Very few people are initially fully comfortable in the company of someone who is blind, deaf, or has cerebral palsy. By acknowledging your discomfort, you can bypass feeling pity, shame, guilt, rejection, or the desire to withdraw. Talk about your discomfort so that your friend might be able to help you deal with it.

Here are a few "messages" to people with disabilities.

- No one can make you feel inferior without your consent.

- If you have interests, someone will be interested in you.

- If you are chronically bored, you will be boring company.

- If you have nothing to do, don't do it in the presence of others.

- Our society does not give points for being handicapped. You need to work hard to make friends and to prove to others that you are a person first and your disability is secondary to everything that is important about you. *You* are not your disability.

Please note: If you know a child with a disability, read *One Miracle at a Time* by Irving Dickman and Sol Gordon (Fireside/Simon & Schuster, 1993), *Beyond a Physical Disability* by Evelyn West Ayrault (Continuum, 2001), or *Doing What Comes Naturally: Dispelling Myths and Fallacies About Sexuality and People with Developmental Disabilities* by Orieda Horn Anderson (High Tide Press, 2000).

Are you someone who tries to please everybody?

Well, no one can. You can only try to keep your own life in order.

You can't please everybody!

What pleases one friend, parent, or teacher may displease another. Your motives and actions are not always understood or appreciated. Therefore, the person that you need to satisfy most is yourself. By being your own person you'll find that some people, but not all (maybe not even many), will like you. Those people who try to please everybody end up pleasing nobody.

Why not just do the best you can? If your best isn't good enough for some people, that's their problem.

What really counts in relationships is intelligence, imagination, integrity, luck, good will, and getting across the impression that you can be trusted.

"Friendship is born at the moment when one person says to another, 'What! You, too? I thought I was the only one.'" —C. S. Lewis

The legitimate purpose of anger is to make a grievance known. If that isn't done appropriately, anger can easily turn into hostility, a desire for revenge, or even violent rage.

Just blowing off steam doesn't result in relief because it isn't considerate of the person at whom the anger is directed.

It is a good idea to count to ten before you express your anger, and sometimes it is a good idea to sit down and ask yourself, "What am I really upset about?"

Are you very angry?

I agree with Carol Travis, who says that if a person does not confront the object of a grievance, it matters little whether that person keeps anger in or lets it out. Those at whom rage is directed also have hurt feelings. Silent sulking, however, is the worst response to someone else's expressions of anger. It's a passive way of expressing hostility, which turns anger inward.

Try to avoid turning your anger into a total rejection of another person. Instead, stick to the issue. Don't say, "I hate you." Say, "I am angry about what you said or what you did."

Anger is a legitimate emotion. However, violence, as Carolyn Swift suggests, is a response of weak, ineffective, inadequate people rather than of effective, strong, competent people.

If you are being repeatedly bullied, and especially if you don't have friends to help you deal with it, you must do everything you can to put an end to it, even if you have to be dramatic and say you won't go to school anymore.

Tell your parents, teacher, principal, counselor, rabbi, or minister that you are afraid of being hurt and that it's up to them to intervene.

Sometimes the worst kind of behavior occurs in a particular place, such as the gym. Insist that something be done. Get a doctor's excuse if necessary. Nobody at school should have to tolerate an unsafe situation.

Are you being teased, bullied, or left out?

Emptiness is a terrible feeling and it gets much worse if you do nothing, sleep a lot, or just mope around. You might:

- Eat too much.

- Drink too much.

- Do drugs.

- Watch too much television.

- Compare yourself to others.

Do you feel empty inside?

These actions don't fill the void and will probably make you feel worse. The only thing that can help is to face reality. This suggestion might make you very anxious, but take heart. The first sign of getting better is feeling anxious. It means that something is there, that you exist.

EMPTY NO LONGER

Take care of yourself. Go for a walk, take a swim, or do another type of exercise. Try to connect with a friend whom you have neglected or a family member whom you haven't seen for some time, even if you think it won't help. Keep on trying.

Talk about what's troubling you with a friend or some person whom you believe you can trust—maybe a parent. Fill the void with ideas, alternatives, faith in the possibility that your circumstances can change. Prayer can help.

You can begin to feel much better, even if nothing changes except that you have made an effort to fill the empty spaces. Since the publication of the first edition of this book, I have received many letters from young people. One of them wrote about her feelings of emptiness. I am reprinting one such letter and my response in the hope that they will help others with similar feelings.

33

Dear Dr. Gordon,

It is 11:04 p.m. and I am trying to fall asleep. I just finished reading your book because my older brother gave it to me off his shelf just 45 minutes ago after I had a talk with him about how I am feeling.

I am fourteen years old and I used to be happy. Just last year I was convinced that I had found myself and I was truly happy. I don't know if I can explain this. I have many friends, am smart in school, and am good at lots of things, but inside I am very unhappy. I don't know how long I've felt this way. It kind of just snuck up on me, but I know it's been around for at least three months.

The way I am is hard to explain. Everyone who knows me will say that I am so happy and I smile all the time. Many of my friends do not understand the emptiness I feel inside, like there's something out there but I don't quite know what I'm looking for. I feel unfulfilled, and though I am surrounded by friends constantly, I feel internally very lonely. I have thought about suicide, though for me it's not an option because I am trying to find life, not get rid of it. I am very confused and overwhelmed by life in general.

I am willing to just live this through if I know it will eventually end. I don't know if I could live with this forever. Maybe one day I will wake up and it will be gone. I hope so. Just taking time to read your book and write this letter has brought up my mood and opened me. Thank you. Please write back.

Susan

34

Dear Susan,

Since my book *When Living Hurts* was first published some years ago, I have received over one thousand letters from young people like you. For the most part, the letters fall into two categories: those that were sent by people (like you) who feel empty inside but are generally perceived by their friends to be happy, and those that were sent by people who have been extremely disappointed by a failed love affair, uncertainty about their sexual orientation, or an inability to get along with their parents. In all instances the underlying problem is a basic anxiety that is revealed in many different ways. People who are disappointed, angry, or confused seem to be unable to separate unfortunate feelings or events from their whole personality. But failure is an event, not a person.

Feeling empty inside is a fairly common problem, and more often than not it is related to a false perception of what life is supposed to be like. Often people like you are seeking the "meaning of life" and don't understand that life is an opportunity, not a meaning. One must enjoy and appreciate the opportunities one has now, at the same time making plans and being hopeful about the future. Things do change and improve (even after a terrible loss, like a death in the family), but this doesn't happen spontaneously, like waking up one morning and finding that everything is fine.

Changes in one's life almost always require a lot of effort and patience. The best way to effect change in your life is to go outside

35

yourself in a sense—to do good deeds and be helpful to others. This is called "mitzvah therapy," because while you are being nice to others, you are also helping yourself. It's amazing how acts of kindness can transform a life. Even just being nice to a person who is lonely, is being picked on, or has no friends can make a big difference in your life. Another way to cope with internal depression is to learn something new. It doesn't matter what it is—learning a new language, a craft, chess, or simply becoming acquainted with a particular author's work. I do recommend that for more suggestions you read my book *A Friend in Need* (Prometheus Books, 2000). If that book doesn't help you, then I recommend you seek counseling to explore some of the inner conflicts that you might be experiencing.

One final note of caution: Approximately 10 percent of the cases of depression have some physical cause. If you often find yourself depressed for no apparent reason, it would be a good idea to get a complete physical examination and tell your doctor about the way you feel. If for any reason the doctor tries to trivialize what you say or makes you feel that you don't know what is going on inside you, he or she is not the right physician for you, and you should look for another.

With best wishes for your personal growth.

Sol Gordon

Looking inward, I see that all too often I fail to use time and talent to improve myself and to serve others. And yet there is in me much goodness and a yearning to use my gifts for the well-being of those around me. This Sabbath [*or* day] calls me to renew my vision, to fulfill the best that is within me. For this I look to God for help.

Meditation

Give meaning to my life and substance to my hopes; help me to understand those around me with the desire to serve them. Let me not forget that I depend on others as they depend on me; quicken my heart and hand to lift them up; make faithful my words of prayer, that they may fulfill themselves in deeds.

—*Gates of Prayer,* (Central Conference of American Rabbis, 1975), p. 188

"The highest form of wisdom is kindness." –*Talmud*

37

Did something terrible happen to you when you were a child?

Although we like to think that children are resilient and flexible, some individuals experience childhood abuse or trauma that causes stress, guilt, or anxiety in later years.

If someone, even someone you cared about, took advantage of you sexually or physically abused you, the first thing you have to remember is that it wasn't your fault, regardless of the circumstances—even if you didn't tell anyone. All mental health specialists agree that when an adult commits such an act, it's never the child's responsibility or fault.

If you had bad thoughts and something happened soon after, remember that your bad thoughts didn't cause the thing to happen. Your thoughts cannot make accidents happen or bring about natural events (like death).

Getting on with your life will not only help you but also those you care about. If you cannot get over your upset or depression, talking about your feelings with a trusted family member, friend, rabbi, counselor, or minister might help you gain a more positive perspective. Sometimes just being understood by someone else is enough to help a person begin developing new attitudes.

Life does not exist without disappointments, upsets, accidents, tragedies, and loss. Everyone who is happy has also been unhappy at some time. If you have never experienced unhappiness, you would have no idea what happiness is.

The most important message: Don't be like the person who abused or hurt you. Don't, as we say in psychology, identify with the aggressor. Remember, the best revenge is living well.

Sometimes "revenge" is the most appropriate response to abuse.

How is that possible?

Once I spoke before a large audience of professionals—about 250 psychiatrists, social workers, counselors, and psychotherapists. They were listening to a lecture I was giving to 30 teenagers at a juvenile detention center. My topic was about love and sex.

At the end of my talk, one teenager posed this question: "Throughout my entire childhood my father beat the hell out of me, no matter how slight the offense. He said he did it because he loved me. I asked a lot of my counselors if they thought that love was my father's motive and they all implied that it probably was, although maybe he overdid it." Then he asked me, "Do you think my father really loved me?" I said no—that's not a way of expressing love. And then he asked me what I thought he should do about it. I replied, "Take revenge!"

The audience responded with outrage and a chorus of disapproval. It was not, of course, a politically correct response. I deliberately waited a couple of minutes and then added, "The best revenge is living well. When you grow up and have children of your own, love them and never hit them."

My rationale was this: how many teenagers appreciate the idea of forgiveness for abuse? So many young people who have been abused grow up to become abusers themselves. This is the history of people who are prone to bullying, domestic violence, and rape. Sometimes the best response to abuse is revenge—but the best revenge is living well. Don't repeat what was done to you.

Living well is the best revenge

39

What was the worst thing that ever happened to you?

What was the worst thing that ever happened to you? Did you learn anything from the experience that could help you now or in the future?

Stop and look at some situations that seem negative or painful. Look at each one from a different angle, as though you were turning a diamond over and over in your hand, examining all its facets.

Remember: every mistake can become a lesson. Even tragic events can become lessons. The ghosts of the past don't have to determine what you can do today. You are in control of your attitude about your feelings. A positive attitude can help change your feelings.

Attitude

by Anonymous

The longer I live, the more I realize the impact of attitude on my life. Attitude to me is more important than facts. It is more important than the past, than education, than money, than circumstances, than failures, than successes, than what other people think or say or do. It is more important than appearance, giftedness, or skill. It will make or break a company, a church, a synagogue, a home. The remarkable thing is you have a choice every day regarding the attitude you will embrace for that day.

We cannot change our past . . . . We cannot change the fact that people will act in a certain way . . . . We cannot change the inevitable. The only thing we can do is play on the one string we have, and that is our attitude.

I am convinced that life is 10 percent what happens to me and 90 percent how I react to it. And so it is with you. YOU are in charge of your attitude.

40

Is it possible that your standards are too high? Unrealistic? Unrealizable? Unreasonable expectations are the main reasons that:

- So many marriages end in divorce.

- So many parents are angry with their children.

- So many children are disappointed in their parents.

- So many love affairs break up.

Think about the following:

WE ALL HAVE OUR LIMITATIONS.

"The wise Rabbi Bunan once said in old age, when he had already grown blind: 'I should not like to change places with our father Abraham! What good would I do God if Abraham became blind like Bunan, and blind Bunan became like Abraham? Rather than this happen, I think I shall try to become a little more myself.'"
—from *The Way of Man*
by Martin Buber

Do most people fall short of your expectations?

41

YOU ARE NOT YOUR THOUGHTS.

YOU ARE WHAT YOU DO.

At times you can get some insights about yourself by examining your thoughts, dreams, and fantasies.

You can use your imagination to write poems and a journal.

Do you have disturbing thoughts?

BUT ONLY WHAT YOU DO WITH YOUR

THOUGHTS DETERMINES WHO YOU ARE.

Remember, *all* thoughts, turn-ons, fantasies, and dreams are normal. They could come to you voluntarily or involuntarily from your unconscious. Although some of them are subject to your control, many are not.

Guilt is the energy for the involuntary repetition of unacceptable thoughts.

If you recognize this, then it doesn't matter how weird or frightening your thoughts are. You will realize that it is normal to have violent thoughts, such as imagining that your friends are dead. You will accept that it is normal to imagine having sex with someone you're not supposed to have sex with. Your thoughts will pass and nothing will happen. Your thoughts will not control you.

But if you allow your thoughts to paralyze you or if you permit them to lead you to violent actions, then your thoughts are not responsible for the outcomes. You are!

42

If you say you can't help having these agonizing thoughts, it may be because you have not yet realized that thoughts of all kinds are normal. Thoughts become abnormal only:

- When they take up most of your time.

- If you respond to them with compulsive or impulsive behavior.

- When they are repressed and then emerge in the form of fears or psychosomatic disorders.

If you want to know more about rational thinking, I recommend that you read *How to Stubbornly Refuse to Make Yourself Miserable about Anything . . . Yes, Anything* by Albert Ellis (Lyle Stuart, Inc., 1988).

It's possible that just by reading this section, you'll feel greatly relieved. Remember the Zen expression, "When the mind is ready, the teacher appears." It is also possible for a bad situation that has lasted for years to change in minutes. Many people have experienced this. It usually is the result of an insight, a love affair, or a useful action. This may not be happening to you right now, but remember that it can happen.

If it has reached the point that your thoughts have become painful, seek help from a counselor, therapist, or clergy person.

43

Friendship

Making friends and, perhaps even more important, having a best friend can be a crucial factor in feeling good about yourself and raising your self-esteem.

In my book *A Friend in Need: How to Help When Times are Tough* (Prometheus Books, 2000), which is, incidentally, my favorite book next to the one you are reading now, I quoted a remark given by Erma Bombeck in a commencement speech: "Most of you are going to be ordinary . . . . You are not going to the moon. You'll be lucky to find the keys to your car in the back parking lot. But some of you are to be great things to yourselves. You are going to be the best friend someone ever had. . . ."

I myself have often felt that my greatest achievements in life have been the friends I've made, more important than my professional accomplishments—especially since I always felt that my Judith, blessed is her memory, was my best friend.

Now here is something to think about. What do you say to this idea? In his book *Love Undetectable* (Knopf, 1998), a brilliant analysis of the history of friendship, Andrew Sullivan describes some advantages of friendship over romance and marriage. The attraction of romantic love, to paraphrase Sullivan, is that it can eclipse every other emotion and transport us to levels of bliss we've never felt before. Love seems eternal, which is why, Sullivan concludes, love is so irresistible and so delusory. The impossibility of love accounts partially for its attraction: "It is an irrational act, a concession to the passions . . . and in almost every regard, friendship delivers what love promises but fails to provide."

Love can often be an issue of control and countercontrol. A condition of friendship is the letting go of power over another person. As soon as a friend attempts to control a friend, the friendship is finished. Abuse of power can end not only traditional friendships, but also love relationships. The core of a love relationship should be a true friendship.

Chapter 2

If You or Someone You Know Is Suicidal

How to get help urgently

It's important to understand that depression can distort your thinking. You may feel stupid even if you have a high IQ. You may feel alone even though you have friends and people who care about you. You may feel empty even if you have dreams and plans. You may feel that nothing can change even though you've been in tough spots before and things did change for the better.

Tell someone you trust that you are depressed and need help. And promise that person you won't harm yourself (even though you've had suicidal thoughts) because you want to give "help" another chance.

After reading this part of the book and any other sections that pertain to your situation, confide in someone about what's troubling you, even if you have to reach out to several people before you get the response that helps you feel better. Speak to a friend or parent first, even if you doubt that person will understand. Then confide in a trustworthy doctor, counselor, teacher, minister, or rabbi, or call a crisis intervention center anytime day or night. Someone there will help you.

If it's someone you know who is in trouble—perhaps someone who you care about has confided in you—

turn immediately to the section *"What to do if someone you care about is suicidal,"* page 55.

If you feel that the danger of suicide is imminent, don't leave the person alone. If possible, you or another person should call the police or a suicide prevention hotline and report that a suicide attempt is in progress (Suicide Hotline 1-800-784-2433). Make sure you give the address and telephone number. Get as close to the person as he or she will allow and say, "Let's talk. For my sake. It's important to me. Please, let's talk. It's possible that I don't understand how you feel. Explain it to me." Try to get the person to discuss possible options and alternatives.

Hands

by Ric Masten

i think of my poems and songs
as hands
if i don't hold them out to you
afraid that you might
laugh at them
spit on them
or totally ignore them
i find i won't be touched

if i keep them in my pocket
i will never get to see you
seeing me
seeing you

and though i know
from experience
many of you
for a myriad of reasons
will laugh
and spit
and walk away unmoved
still
to meet those of you
who do reach out
is well worth the risk
and pain

so
here are my hands
do what you will

How to help someone who is in a panic or having what's sometimes called an anxiety attack

Anxiety is experienced as an overwhelming state of tension or fear (often the result of the anticipation of some unknown danger or of not being able to handle a scheduled task or performance), which should not be confused with normal stress or tension before an event. Anxiety attacks may be accompanied by certain physical reactions, such as a rapid heartbeat, sweating, trembling, nausea, and difficulty with normal breathing,* in addition to intense fears of losing control, going crazy, and even dying.

Here's what to do when someone is having such an attack. Say something like, "Listen, you are having an anxiety attack. If you've had one before, you know you'll get over it. If it's the first time, it's very scary. But it is not dangerous and it will pass. [How do you know? the person asks.] I read about it in a book. [What causes it?] It's not important to discuss that now.

"Here's what you are supposed to do. Sit down, close your eyes, and tense up. Then relax every part of your body. Start with your toes, feet, legs. . . ." (Progressively name the other body parts and suggest that the person visualize those body parts in his or her mind.)

"I'll stay with you. I know that all kinds of ideas will come into your mind. This is common. It happens to a lot of people. [How do you know?] It was clearly

---

* If the person is panting and out of breath, one way to help him or her breathe normally is to have the person place a small paper bag around the nose and mouth and breath into the bag until the panting stops. Breathing the same air over and over for three or four minutes helps the person control the panting by restoring the carbon dioxide in the blood to normal levels, calming the person down.

stated in a psychology book that I read. What you are going through is not comfortable and may even be terrifying, but it is *not*, I repeat, *not* dangerous."

Stay as calm as you can for your own sake and your friend's. It's okay to be scared in a crisis. Just know your limits and know when to get help.

Other anxiety reducers are exercise, yoga, meditation, a hot bath, and drinking a cup of herbal tea.

Please note: These are first aid procedures. Don't try to talk a person out of the anxiety attack by suggesting that it's nothing to worry about. Nor will the relaxation approach solve the basic problem. If intense physical pain is present, emergency medical help may be needed. If you do suspect that it is an anxiety attack, suggest that the person talk with a counselor or psychiatrist at a later time.

KNOWING WHAT TO DO

TO HELP SOMEONE IN TROUBLE

IS A GOOD FEELING.

Are you sometimes depressed? *Everybody* gets depressed occasionally. Almost all such depressions are normal. Have you ever thought about suicide? Did you know that almost everyone has?

Do you know someone who has killed himself or herself? Isn't it painful to recall or visualize that person? Wouldn't you like to be in a position to help someone (perhaps even yourself) who is seriously considering committing suicide?

Dying to live the good life?

Most people who think about or actually commit suicide do so in response to feelings of depression or despair. They have not learned how to deal with disappointments. They may feel ashamed about something they've done. They feel that there is no way out of their situation or that their agony will last forever. They feel that no one believes in or understands them. For them, life is no longer meaningful. Many of these people haven't grasped the fact that life without frustrations, depressions, and profound periods of mourning simply doesn't exist. People who commit suicide look at life as bleak and black. They sometimes expect perfection of themselves in a very intense way. But mostly they find it inconceivable to imagine that

- Things can always change.

- They have many options.

Many experts claim they can tell if a person is suicidal, but they can't. Every person is unique, as are the reasons for suicide. What we can say with certainty is that every statement of suicidal intent is a cry for help, as is every suicide attempt.

Anyone who is suicidal requires professional help and, sometimes, antidepressant medication. But psychiatrists, psychologists, and social workers can't "cure" a depressed person without the help of that person's friends and family.

The following is a bit of personal philosophy of life that I have found can be helpful.

- Don't go around looking for *the* meaning of life. Look for an opportunity to have meaningful experiences.

- Disappointments are a part of everybody's life.

- If you don't expect miracles to occur in your life, you won't notice them when they happen.

- The first miracle takes place when you stop comparing yourself to others.

Miracles

Why, who makes much of a miracle?
As to me I know of nothing else but miracles,
Whether I walk the streets of Manhattan,
Or dart my sight over roofs of houses toward the sky,
Or wade with naked feet along the beach just in the edge of the water,
Or stand under the trees in the woods,
Or talk by day with any one I love, or sleep in the bed at night with any one I love,
Or sit at table at dinner with the rest,
Or look at strangers opposite me riding in the car,

53

Or watch honey-bees busy around the hive of a
summer forenoon,
Or animals feeding in the fields,
Or birds, or the wonderfulness of insects in the air,
Or the wonderfulness of the sundown, or of stars
shining so quiet and bright,
Or the exquisite delicate thin curve of the new moon
in spring;
These with the rest, one and all, are to me miracles,
The whole referring, yet each distinct and in
its place.

To me every hour of the light and dark is a miracle,
Every cubic inch of space is a miracle,
Every square yard of the surface of the earth is
spread with the same,
Every foot of the interior swarms with the same.

To me the sea is a continual miracle,
The fishes that swim—the rocks—the motion of the
waves—the ships with men in them,
What stranger miracles are there?

—Walt Whitman, from *Leaves of Grass*

If someone you care about is suicidal, listen to that person. Don't argue or attempt to prove that what he or she is planning to do doesn't make sense. Respond by saying things like:

- It must be so painful for you.

- As long as you are alive, things can change.

- I'll help and always stick by you.

- I care about you.

Don't say:

- You're being silly (*or* stupid).

- Let's forget about it.

- Let's have some fun.

- Let's go to a movie or a dance.

Don't suggest taking a drink or drugs. Lowering inhibitions and muddying thinking can make a person reckless and can possibly lead to suicide.

Don't be afraid to talk with your friend or brother or sister about what he or she is thinking or planning to do. You might ask, "Have you ever felt as though life's not worth living?" You will not be putting ideas into the person's head. On the contrary, if the person is considering suicide, it's good for him or her to talk about it. *Direct questions about suicidal intent do not provoke suicidal behavior*. Ask the person, "Have you ever wished you were dead?" "Are you thinking of suicide?" "Are there some things you've thought about or done that you've never told anyone?" Then find out how urgent the crisis is. Ask: "How do you plan to kill yourself?" "Have you been thinking about dying for some time now?" "When do you think you'll kill yourself?"

What to do if someone you care about is suicidal

55

If the crisis is urgent* (if the person knows how he or she plans to die, has the means, and is ready to act), *do not leave the person*. Take him or her to a parent, a counselor, a minister, a rabbi, a suicide prevention clinic, or whatever support system seems best at the time. If the person refuses to meet with anyone, secretly call someone for help. *Try not to bear the burden of the responsibility alone*.

Any expressed suicidal intent or inference should be taken seriously. Inferences might include comments like:

- I won't be around much longer.
- Soon nobody will have to worry about me.
- I have nothing to live for.
- Nothing works for me.
- I'm a loser.
- They'll be sorry when I'm gone.

If the expressions of suicide seem serious but not urgent, talk with the person and really listen to find out what's troubling him or her.

Usually something has happened in that person's life to cause a serious crisis. Among the possibilities are rejection by a lover, the death of a close family member, an impending divorce, or the loss of employment.

It doesn't matter if *you* think what the person is upset about is trivial. It's how the person feels that counts.

Accept the feelings that are being expressed. Don't tell the person not to worry. Don't minimize the

* In any suicidal emergency, call 911 or 1-800-SUICIDE (784-2433) if you need help.

event by saying things like "You'll get over it" or "It's nothing" or "You think you have troubles?" Don't try to coax the person out of the hurt he or she feels.

Do:

- Be a friend and empathize.

- Be sad with the person.

- Give the person a hug.

- Take the person for a walk.

- Jog together.

- Exercise together.

- Suggest the person talk to a therapist.

Stay with the person as long as possible. Make a definite appointment for your next visit. Say: "Call me anytime—even in the middle of the night." Go out for a meal or an ice cream. The act of sharing a meal can lift depression, if only for a short time. Make a pact with your friend—what he or she will do, what you will do, when you will meet—and compare notes. Let your friend know you will see him or her through this.

Show that you care. Everybody needs someone who believes in him or her.

Don't:

- Take the person to parties or anyplace where people are having fun. (Most really sad people become even more depressed when they are around people who are having a good time.)

- Try to give easy answers or solve the person's problems for him or her.

57

- Ask your friend, "Is this the worst thing that's ever happened?"

- Tell lies like, "She (he) really does love you," or "Everybody is your friend."

- Put the person on a heavy religious guilt trip.

Don't say things like, "You have everything going for you." Instead, respond with such caring messages as "If you think I don't know how you feel, tell me more so I can understand better."

And tell your friend how much you would feel the loss of his or her presence in your life. The main thing is for you to encourage your friend to talk, reveal his or her thoughts, and confide in you.

Doctors can help in dealing with depression. In some crisis situations, medications can result in almost immediate relief. What doesn't work is blame, resentment, or hostility.

Earl A. Grollman cautions in his excellent book *Suicide* (updated ed., Beacon Press, 1988) that the suicidal person is already suffering from a burden of "punishing guilt feelings." If that person is told by society and religion that suicide is immoral, his or her guilt and depression may increase. For the suicidal person, Grollman says, suicide isn't a theological issue but the result of terrible emotional stress. The main thing is for you to encourage your friend to talk, reveal his or her thoughts, and confide in you.

Nobody ever fully recovers from the death of a child, a close friend, or a sibling who commits suicide. It is difficult not to be haunted by a dreadful sense of having done something wrong or of having failed to do something right.

So many people who commit, try to commit, or even think about suicide do so because they feel a sense of hopelessness and sometimes a sense that life is without purpose or meaning. They may feel that threatening to kill themselves is heroic.

But it is not heroic. It shows a failure to connect meaningfully with people who might or would like to love and believe in them.

Keep in mind: Suicide is a permanent solution to a temporary problem.

If you are told in confidence that someone you care about is considering suicide, should you tell anyone? Yes!

Find a way to tell the person's parents, spouse, counselor, minister, or rabbi that you are worried. The more worried you are, the more explicit you should be.

Do not keep a suicidal intent confidential

That is not easy. Sometimes the best you can do isn't enough. You can't always trust your own judgment about whether the threat of suicide is serious or not.

You could easily be thinking that

- The person is not the type.
- The person is carrying on or is just using suicide as an attention-getting device.
- You don't believe the person is serious.
- The person seems much better now.

Many people commit suicide after their depression has lifted and they have regained the energy to go through with the suicide. A person may have already decided to commit suicide and, therefore, comes across as very calm, as if he or she has nothing more to worry about. *This calm period is a dangerous time and is a signal.*

If your friend refuses to get help, you might start by calling a crisis center. Give your friend this book to read. Encourage him or her to talk to another close friend or relative.

Please realize that nobody expects you to be the therapist and resolve the problem. At the same time, you may be the only person your friend confides in and, therefore, the only person who can help. By determining the seriousness of the crisis, motivating the person to seek help, and showing your support, you can make a difference.

If the person says to you, "Leave me alone," you should be aware that he or she seldom means it.

THE CRUCIAL POINT FOR YOU
TO UNDERSTAND IS THAT
SUICIDAL INTENT
CAN BE REVERSED.

In addition to the factors presented above, many suicidal people haven't learned how to cope with disappointments and depressions. We live in a society that values instant gratification. When people feel bad, they often take a pill or a drink or do something to try to escape how they feel. If they can't get relief right away, they might be overcome by despair. Everybody has to learn to cope with disappointments and even tragic happenings. That's part of living. A bad situation does not always resolve itself as quickly as we would like, and it's easy to become discouraged. However, everything does eventually change, especially if we work at it. If someone we love doesn't understand this, it's up to us to convince that person. There is no greater mitzvah* than to save a life.

> *"Although the world is full of suffering, it is also full of the overcoming of it."*
> —*Helen Keller*

---

* *Mitzvah* is a Hebrew word that means "commandment" but is often used to mean "good deed."

You can't always tell the difference between a cry for help and depression, but here are some points to consider.

Francine Klagsbrun, in her excellent book for parents and counselors called *Too Young to Die—Youth and Suicide* (Houghton Mifflin, 1976), writes:

Friends, relatives, teachers, coworkers . . . make up the front line of defense against suicide . . . . And they must help, even if they believe the suicidal person is manipulating them or using threats of suicide to gain attention. A person who must resort to suicide to get attention has lost the ability to communicate in normal ways. The person needs attention. Without it the next cry for help will be shriller, more desperate, more dangerous.

Can you tell the difference between a cry for help, a wish for attention, and depression?

Erring on the side of caution is better than being sorry later.

There are two main kinds of suicide: the impulsive kind that ends a life and the slow, not entirely intentional kind that often produces equally grim results. The second kind may include:

- Driving while intoxicated
- Drug addiction
- Alcoholism
- Fasting
- Eating too much (especially if self-induced vomiting follows a binge)
- Smoking
- Suicide attempts
- Sexual promiscuity
- Violence and crime
- Retreating into despair

These possible suicide warning signs could also indicate depression, extreme anxiety, physical illness, or a temporary, and even appropriate, response to loss. They include:

- The expression of feelings of hopelessness and despair

- Incommunicative behavior

- Self mutilation

- Explosive outbursts

- A loss of appetite or excessive eating

- A loss of interest in activities once considered enjoyable

- A loss of energy or extreme fatigue

- Relentless pacing

- Sleeplessness

- A preoccupation with the idea that "nobody understands" or "I have no friends"

- Talk about death or suicide

- Moodiness and sudden bursts of crying

- Increased isolation from friends and family

- A tendency to become more active and aggressive than usual (unlike suicidal adults, who tend to become apathetic when severely depressed)

- A serious drop in grades for those still in school

- The giving away of valued possessions

- A morbid sense of shame

Possible suicide warning signs

63

- An increased interest in getting his or her "life in order"
- A sudden and intense interest in religious beliefs and the afterlife
- A profound emotional response to a recent loss, such as a divorce or death in the family, or a good friend's moving away
- A previous suicide attempt
- A deep sense of loneliness

Even though the vast majority of people who exhibit one or more of the above signs will not attempt to commit suicide or become mentally ill, these signs do represent, for the most part, *changes* in behavior that warrant serious concern.

Here is something to think about:

In some cases you may find yourself in the position of having to get direct help for someone who is suicidal and refuses to go for counseling. If so, do it. Don't be afraid of appearing disloyal. Many people who are suicidal have given up hope. They no longer believe they can be helped. They feel it is useless. The truth is, they can be helped. With time, most suicidal people can be restored to full and happy living. But when they are feeling hopeless, their judgment is impaired. They can't see a reason to go on living. In that case, it is up to you to use your judgment to see that they get the help they need. What at the time may be an act of disloyalty or the breaking of a confidence could turn out to be the favor of a lifetime. Your courage and willingness to act could save a life.

—Excerpted from *Suicide in Youth and What You Can Do About It*. Prepared by the Suicide Prevention and Crisis Center of San Mateo County, California, in cooperation with the American Association of Suicidology and Merck Sharp and Dohme.

"Whoever preserves one life, it is if he preserved an entire world."

—Talmud

See the Resources section for helpful addresses, telephone numbers, and Web sites.

65

Why are so many young people killing them- selves?

We don't really know why so many young people kill themselves. We do know that the suicide rate among young people between the ages of 15 and 24 has tripled in the past 30 years, resulting in between 5,000 and 6,000 deaths a year. In fact, suicide is the third leading cause of death in this age group, after accidents and murder. In addition, several hundred thousand young people make serious suicide attempts every year.

Most experts agree that the following are characteristics of suicide:

- Depression or a feeling of hopelessness is the most important cause of suicide (in my judgment not always true for teenagers).

- Almost all suicides are preventable.

- Many people who took their own lives had made it known in some way that they were intending to do so. Suicide attempts of any kind should always be considered a "cry for help."

- Almost all suicidal people have mixed feelings about the act: They want to do it and they don't. Suicide is something impulsive, but it may also be an act of desperation or the result of a desire for revenge.

- Suicide is often the culmination of a long period of multiple difficulties (and the result of the ready availability of a gun or drugs).

Young people need to know that however intolerable the emotion or unendurable the pain, it will pass. It will change. It is temporary. As long as the person is alive, there is time for everything, including finding out why he or she wanted to die.

You may not know whether life is worth living or not until you've lived for a good while. When you are forty, you will be able to reexamine what has happened to you. Then you can ask yourself the ultimate question: Has it been worth it?

Strange as it may seem to you now, in almost all cases people answer yes.

Whatever age you are, living requires courage.

What if you think that life isn't worth living?

"Courage is the ability to dispose of self-pity and wallowing. You have to look beyond yourself. Courage is not, in any way, self-centered except it is self-confident. The most courageous person says, 'It's okay. I can beat this.'"

—*Monica Dickens*

Research by Jan Alan Fawcett, M.D. (Professor of Psychiatry, Rush Presbyterian St. Luke's Medical Center) suggests that symptoms like severe anxiety, panic attacks, diminished concentration, and profound loss of interest or ability to experience pleasure seem to be significant predictors of the early onset of suicide attempts. Dr. Fawcett makes a special point of stating that severe anxiety and other related symptoms can be alleviated if they are recognized and treated.

Why teens commit suicide

It is generally agreed among health specialists that untreated clinical depression* is the number one cause of suicide. About 31,000 Americans commit suicide each year. About 5,000 are between the ages of 15 to 24.

According to the National Strategy for Suicide Prevention (U.S. Department of Health and Human Services, 2001), each year 650,000 people receive emergency care after attempting to take their own lives. Suicide is a major public health problem. It is one of the top 10 leading causes of death in the United States, ranking eighth or ninth in the last few decades. In addition to 31,000 suicide deaths per year, there are an estimated 200,000 individuals who will be affected by the loss of a loved one.

In my judgment and experience, untreated clinical depression alone does not account for the reasons a majority of young people between the ages of 15 and 24 kill themselves. Youths who attempt or commit suicide generally come from middle class homes and have caring parents. Prior to suicide they revealed no apparent mental illness or brain damage and were not known to abuse alcohol or drugs—however much they appeared to their parents to be extra sensitive or just plain unlucky to find themselves in vulnerable circumstances.

Some circumstances, which are taken from actual cases, were:

- Being victimized by a bully for the first time.

- Being harassed by a vindictive teacher (perhaps for the first time).

- Being extremely happy for months after having fallen in love (madly) for the first time, then killed

---

* Clinical depression is considered a mental illness, rarely observed and diagnosed before the age of twenty. The cause is often in dispute.

themselves after being "jilted." (Perhaps believing the common myth that you can only *really* fall in love once.)

- Having counted all their lives on being accepted to a prestigious college or being accepted for pilot training upon entering the Air Force, but being rejected.

- Being arrested for stealing or a minor crime.

- Being worried about being a homosexual.

- Experiencing the death of a parent or close friend.

- Being abused, which triggered memories of an abusive past.

Suicide, often an impulsive act, is made "easier" in these circumstances by the ready access to guns and drugs.

Prior to these circumstances, none of the cases cited were considered to be suicidal. Oddly enough, there is some evidence to suggest that even those who failed to kill themselves were not diagnosed afterward as mentally ill. Many have gone on to lead "successful" lives, however this may be interpreted.

That's why most of the interventions cited in this book are for young people who are not known to have been identified as mentally ill, brain damaged, or leading an addictive lifestyle. This is not to say that we should not be alert to the symptoms of clinical depression, which may be a factor in some teenage suicides.

These are the signs considered by experts to be evidence of teen depression (not just sadness) which would require psychiatric intervention. (This list is proposed by Karen I. Swartz, M.D. in an article in *The Prevention Researcher* [Nov. 2001, vol. 8, no. 4]).

Symptoms of Teenage Depression:

· Depressed or irritable mood

· Decreased interest or pleasure in activities

· Change in appetite or weight

· Sleeping more or less than usual

· Feeling restless or slowed down

· Fatigue or loss of energy

· Feelings of guilt or worthlessness

· Decreased concentration

· Sense of hopelessness

· Substance abuse

· Recurrent thoughts of death or suicide

Dr. Swartz suggests that in order to make the diagnosis of major depression, five or more of these symptoms must be present for two weeks.

Risk factors for suicide (according to The National Strategy for Suicide Prevention, a 2001 report prepared by the Surgeon General[*]):

Biopsychosocial risk factors:

· Mental disorders, particularly mood disorders, schizophrenia, anxiety disorders, and certain personality disorders

· Alcohol and other substance abuse disorders

· Hopelessness

· Impulsive and/or aggressive tendencies

· History of trauma or abuse

[*] Copies available free by calling 1-800-789-2647.

- Some major physical illnesses
- Previous suicide attempt
- Family history of suicide

Environmental risk factors:

- Job or financial loss
- Relational or social loss
- Easy access to lethal means
- Local clusters of suicide that have a contagious influence

Sociocultural risk factors:

- Lack of social support and sense of isolation
- Stigma associated with help-seeking behavior
- Barriers to accessing health care, especially mental health and substance abuse treatment
- Certain cultural and religious beliefs (for instance, the belief that suicide is a noble resolution of a personal dilemma)
- Exposure to, including through the media, and influence of others who have died by suicide

This report is the research that I generally favor, with some reservations. It contains an excellent prevention strategy, although it does not pay sufficient attention to the crucial aspect of sex education. Almost one-third of the young people who committed suicide are thought to have done so because of concerns about their sexuality. It appears to me that these young people had not "come out" as gay, but rather that they were among those who are

71

fearful that they *might* be homosexual, or have been harassed and identified as such by bullies. Most had probably never had a homosexual experience, or were involved in only a single incident. Or they might have been abused in childhood. (This is an assumption— no direct evidence.) Mostly they worry because of persistent fantasies. They are not aware that all thoughts are normal. Guilt is the energy or mechanism that causes fantasies to be repetitive. The thoughts become agonizing and then are deemed "proof" that they must be valid.

My work challenges the suicide prevention establishment, but only with reference to suicide of young people between the ages of 15 to 24. And I emphasize that the presence of a gun in the home is one of the strongest predictors of "successful" teenage suicide.

Special Note for Young People Reading this Book: Yes, bad things happen to good people. No matter how bad the offense, people recover. They get better. Almost every young person who has attempted suicide is glad that he or she didn't succeed. Give life a chance and the people who care about you a chance to help you.

Please read the following special appeal from a bereaved mother.

Please Promise Me
That You Won't Do Anything
to Hurt Yourself

A letter from a bereaved mother

I spoke with one of the leading suicide researchers in the country about two weeks before my son decided to take his own life. He told me that the most important intervention for severely depressed persons was to get them to promise not to do anything to hurt themselves. I didn't use that intervention with my son because I was totally unaware that he might become suicidal. So that my son may not have totally died in vain, I am asking *you* to please promise me that *you* won't do anything to hurt yourself. It is depression that is distorting your thinking. My son wrote that he was stupid at a time when he was being elected to Phi Beta Kappa. My son said that he was lonely, that he had alienated almost everyone. My son was revered by many. Depression brings distorted thinking.

My son was a kind, concerned, and thoughtful person. I can't believe that he would have wanted to cause pain to so many people. He wouldn't have wanted to spoil graduation for his housemates or his girlfriend. My son said he felt guilty

73

about the cost of his education and the sacrifice that it entailed. Not graduating, not fulfilling any promise after graduation was certainly not a rational solution to irrational guilt. I'm sure my son would not have wanted any one of the thousands of ordinary situations to cause me remorse and pain—searing, sharp, horrid pain. I'm sure that my son would not have wanted to destroy elderly and sick grandparents. My son made a grievous error. You can make a better choice. *Please, please promise me that you won't do anything to hurt yourself or anyone else by rash impulse or distorted thought.* If I sound desperate, I am. I can't imagine that my sensitive, accomplished son would have wanted to harm his friends and family.

Help and relief will eventually come. A friend of my son had a major depression. She tried to hurt herself and failed. She got treatment. She is now well. It might take time, but you will get well, too. In the meantime, your promising not to hurt yourself is the only consolation I can have. Please help to console me. Promise me that if you have out-of-control feelings, you'll call 911 or call a hospital. Right now, find someone to call, and write that number down. Put it where

you can easily find it at any time. I know
the world is full of answering machines.
If you plan now, you can help to save
yourself if the need arises. Remember, I
am counting on it. Thank you.

Author's note: In case it's not absolutely clear from
the above letter, medical management of clinical
depression should begin as soon as symptoms
are apparent.

75

My deep concern for young people who are experiencing suicidal thoughts prompts me to include the following suggestions from parents and friends of people who committed suicide, taken from Iris Bolton's book *My Son . . . My Son . . . A Guide to Healing after Death, Loss, or Suicide* (12th ed., Bolton Press, 1991). The suggestions may help you decide to get help. If your concern is for someone else, the insights of these survivors might assist you in determining the best way to help that person.

Suggestions for survivors by Iris Bolton

- Know that you can survive. You may not think so, but you can.

- Struggle with why it happened until you know you no longer need to know why or until you are satisfied with partial answers.

- Know that you may feel overwhelmed by the intensity of your feelings, but all your feelings are normal.

- Anger, guilt, confusion, and forgetfulness are common responses. You are not crazy. You are in mourning.

- Be aware that you may feel appropriate anger at the person, at the world, at God, at yourself. It's okay to express your feelings.

- You may feel guilty for what you think you did or did not do. Guilt can turn into regret, through forgiveness.

- Having suicidal thoughts is common. It does not mean that you will act on those thoughts.

- Remember to take one moment or one day at a time.

- Find a good listener with whom you can share your thoughts. Call someone if you need to talk.

- Don't be afraid to cry. Tears are healing.

- Give yourself time to heal.

- Remember, the choice was not yours. No one is the sole influence in another's life.

- Expect setbacks. If emotions return like a tidal wave, you may only be experiencing a remnant of grief, an unfinished piece.

- Try to put off major decisions.

- Give yourself permission to get professional help.

- Be aware of the pain of your family and friends.

- Be patient with yourself and with others who may not understand.

- Set your own limits and learn to say no.

- Steer clear of people who want to tell you *what* or *how* to feel.

- Know there are support groups that can be helpful, such as Compassionate Friends or Survivors of Suicide groups. If not, ask a professional to help start one.

- Call on your personal faith to help you through.

- It is common to experience physical reactions to your grief (e.g., headaches, loss of appetite, inability to sleep).

- The willingness to laugh with others and at yourself is healing.

- Wear out your questions, anger, guilt, or other feelings until you can let them go. Letting go doesn't mean forgetting.

- Know that you will never be the same again, but you can survive and even go beyond just surviving.

77

Sex and Love: Worries and Facts

Are you worried about sex?

This section is written for teenagers and young adults, but everyone, including parents, can profit from it.

I'm not sure that most teenagers are mature enough to have sexual intercourse. Many are too young, too vulnerable, too easily exploitable. About 60 percent of teenagers don't use contraceptives the first time they have sex. They don't realize that a person's first experience of sex is usually unsatisfying. (Seldom does a girl have an orgasm; a boy gets his only three days later when he tells the guys about it.) But if you are going to have sex anyway, use protection. It's not romantic to just let it happen. It's stupid. By the way, this applies to oral sex as well, as oral sex can also result in sexually transmitted diseases.

Remember, most young people who talk about their sexual experiences are boasting at someone else's expense.

Special alert for girls: If a guy says, "If you really love me, you'll have sex with me," it's almost always a line and he will probably abandon you, usually the next day.

79

Current studies reveal that almost one in five high school girls has been physically, emotionally, or sexually abused by a dating partner. These girls are more likely to become victims of unintended pregnancy, venereal disease, drug addiction, and suicide attempts.

At the first sign of bullying or abuse, terminate the relationship—no matter what he says or threatens. No form of sexual or physical abuse should be tolerated.

AIDS (Acquired Immunodeficiency Syndrome) is the late stage of an infection caused by HIV (Human Immunodeficiency Virus). This virus damages the immune system, leaving a person susceptible to infections and some cancers. As of this writing, AIDS is still a fatal disease, although currently available medication is now able to prolong life for many years.

It could take as long as ten years before a person infected with the virus acquires AIDS. It does appear that not everyone with an HIV-positive diagnosis will develop full-blown AIDS, but everyone who is positive can infect other people by engaging in unprotected sex or sharing unclean needles, like those used for injecting drugs. Infected women who become pregnant can also pass on the virus to their babies.

HIV is mainly transmitted by sexual contact. In the United States it originally affected mostly gay and bisexual men who had engaged in anal intercourse, as well as intravenous drug users. Today it is just as common to get infected through heterosexual sex. Now HIV is spreading rapidly through heterosexual intercourse in many countries of the world, especially those in Asia and Africa. Worldwide, AIDS is considered the worst plague in the history of humankind. Some 40 million men, women, and children are suffering from HIV, almost all without treatment. Currently in the United States, one out of five people with AIDS is in his or her twenties. These people were probably exposed to the virus in their teens.

HIV organisms are usually found in semen, vaginal fluids, and the blood of infected people.

AIDS alert and STD (sexually transmitted disease) cautions

Unless both people in a sexual relationship (regardless of sexual orientation) are monogamous, honest, and absolutely certain about the other's sexual history, the practice of safer sex is essential. This includes the use of latex condoms with spermicide containing Nonoxynol-9 and the avoidance of anal or oral sex. Sex with multiple partners or prostitutes should also be avoided. In order for the virus to spread, there must be transmission of bodily fluids (that is, semen, vaginal fluids, and/or blood), so don't let such fluids enter your body. Even safer sex is not 100 percent safe. Deep kissing, sexual massage, and mutual masturbation fall into the category of safer sex. HIV is not transmitted by casual contact like holding hands or hugging.

If you are concerned about having been exposed, get an HIV antibody test. Any health department will inform you about the location of confidential testing sites. Get retested as often as health care providers suggest. If you prove to be HIV positive, you *must* seek medical guidance and counseling. Be sure to inform all sexual partners, past and present, about your condition.

What are the symptoms of AIDS?

At first, AIDS symptoms can resemble common illnesses such as cold and stomach flu. Some of the symptoms are:

· Persistent or chronic diarrhea

· Fever, chills, or night sweats

· Extreme weight loss

- Swollen glands on the neck or under the arms
- Purple, pink, or brown spots on the body
- White spots or sores in the mouth
- A dry cough or shortness of breath
- Memory loss or confusion

If you have any of these or other unusual symptoms, consult a doctor or a nurse who knows about AIDS. If you don't know where to go, call your local hot line. The AIDS hot line number is 1-800-342-AIDS or 1-800-344-7432 in Spanish.

AIDS or an unwanted pregnancy are not your only worries when it comes to unprotected sex. And there is more to worry about than the sexually transmitted diseases you hear about most, like syphilis (about 70,000 cases annually) or gonorrhea (about 650,000 cases annually). Do you know about chlamydia? Almost half of the 3 million people infected with chlamydia each year do not have initial symptoms, but if the disease is left untreated, it can cause sterility. There is also PID (Pelvis Inflammatory Disease)—420,000 cases—and genital herpes— one million cases each year (still without a cure and hard to diagnose in women). Also going around are genital warts, hepatitis C, and hepatitis B (for which there is an immunization, but only about 10 percent of sexually active people bother to be immunized). A recent report concluded that 15 million new sexually transmitted infections occur each year, almost two-thirds of them contracted by people under age 25, and one-quarter by teenagers.

So don't have sex without a latex condom and a female form of birth control. Don't be persuaded by a male partner's argument that he hardly gets any feelings when he uses a condom. If he says this, the female partner should reply, "Then you won't get any feelings at all." It's your health that is at stake.

For more information about sexually transmitted diseases, call the National STD Hotline at 1-800-227-8922.

All thoughts, wishes, dreams, fantasies, sexual turn-ons, no matter how weird, are normal. Often these feelings come from the primitive unconscious, and we have no control over them. If you recognize this fact, such thoughts of yours will pass and nothing will happen. If you feel guilty about your fantasies, they will probably recur. *Remember, guilt is the energy that fuels the repetition of unacceptable ideas.* They could become obsessive and cause unacceptable behavior, such as rape, sexual molestation, and preoccupation with pornography. Remember, all sexual thoughts and turn-ons are okay, but exploitive behavior is not. It's all right to think about sexual seduction, but it's not acceptable to exploit someone.

Of course, the ultimate fantasy is to fall in love with someone whose fantasy is to fall in love with you. This sometimes happens in reality. The ultimate turn-on is getting to know, trust, and become intimate with someone you love.

Sexual fantasies

Mastur-bation

Many sad, depressed, anxious young people worry about masturbation. They don't know that masturbation is a healthy, normal expression of sexuality for both males and females. It is not physically harmful no matter how frequently you do it. (Males do not use up their supply of sperm, which is replenished and available all their lives.) A person can, however, live a healthy, normal life without ever having masturbated. If you feel guilty about masturbation or if you don't like it, don't do it. But it's normal. Almost all males and most females masturbate.

Voluntary behavior is the best kind. For example, eating is normal, but if people eat too much to somehow address an emotional problem (and not because they are hungry), eating becomes involuntary, or compulsive. Masturbation can be the same way. It is healthy and normal to masturbate voluntarily. When masturbation becomes compulsive, and you feel as though you have no choice but to masturbate, you might have some other emotional problems that should be addressed in a healthier way. While it is true that no one ever died of over-masturbating, compulsive masturbation can be as dangerous and disastrous as compulsive eating, drinking, or gambling. If you are concerned about compulsive masturbation, you can find help at a local Sexaholics Anonymous group (see the Appendix for contact information), or read the book *Out of the Shadows: Understanding Sexual Addiction* by Patrick J. Carnes (Hazeldon Information Services, 2001).

Really great orgasms can be achieved by masturbating (and fantasizing at the same time), if you do so without guilt. Masturbation can be relaxing and has no harmful side effects. But if you feel guilty about masturbating, you'll find that it will increase tension instead of reducing it. If you have an impulse to hurt or exploit someone or yourself in a sexual way, masturbate instead (privately, creatively, and with lubrication), and you'll be surprised how quickly your impulse will disappear. The impulse may reappear, but you now know what to do about it. If masturbation bothers you or you feel that you are not in control, get counseling. While masturbation itself is not harmful or bad, it may not solve problems you are experiencing. You still need to work out your problems.

For more information about masturbation, read *The Big Book of Masturbation* by Martha Cornog (Down There Press, 2003).

Homo-sexuality

We don't know why certain people are homosexual, but we do know that homosexuality is *not* a disease or a disorder. Recent clinical evidence suggests that some people are born homosexual. Some scientists think it is a trait that develops very early in life. Others maintain that both a genetic predisposition and early development play a role in a human being's sexual orientation. Some people say they knew that they were homosexual at a very early age. Sexual orientation by its very nature cannot be taught, nor can a person's appearance convey whether he or she is homosexual. Most gay men are not feminine, and most lesbians are not masculine. Femininity in males and masculinity in females are not necessarily characteristics of homosexuality.

The majority of intelligent and sexually mature people are aware that they have both homosexual and heterosexual thoughts and feelings at some time during their lives and that these are quite normal occurrences. Childhood and adolescent attraction to members of one's own sex are not uncommon, just as having homosexual thoughts or dreams does not necessarily mean that a person is gay or lesbian.

Gay men and lesbians have existed in every culture and society. Some societies accept the incidence of homosexuality as natural, while others label it abnormal.

Homosexuals exist in every strata of society—among the rich and poor, the educated and uneducated. They work in every imaginable profession. They are doctors, lawyers, politicians, police officers, mechanics, hairdressers, construction workers, athletes, and artists. Think what the world would be like without the work of Melissa Etheridge, Ellen Degeneres, Rufus Wainwright, Nathan Lane, Boy George, Elton John, Freddie Mercury, Michelangelo, Andy Warhol, k. d. lang, Keith Haring, Martina Navratilova, Rosie O'Donnell, Cecil Beaton, Tchaikovsky, Diaghilev, Walt Whitman, Oscar Wilde, E. M. Forster, Gertrude Stein, Truman Capote, James Baldwin, and Bayard Rusten.

Homophobia can make life difficult for gays and lesbians. Still, most homosexuals, like other people who are discriminated against, adjust and become productive members of society. Many find love and companionship with lifelong partners.

If you have decided that you are homosexual, one of the most difficult issues you will face is whether to let people know. If parents and friends react with understanding, coming out can strengthen these important relationships. But there are some cautions about coming out. First of all, you must realize that parents who discover that their child is gay or lesbian are often concerned. They might say something like, "Where did I go wrong?" or "It's just a phase; you'll grow out of it" or "You're sick; you need a psychiatrist." If you know what to expect, you can prepare yourself to be patient and to teach them some of the facts about homosexuality.

Before you come out to your friends and peers, be sure to think about the probable reactions of those closest to you. Consider whether they can be trusted with this most personal information. Your sexual identity is your own business, and you have the right to be as protective of yourself as you think is

89

necessary. Some parents and friends may not understand and may overreact. Of course, whether or not your friends and family accept your sexual orientation, you need to feel good about yourself. Perhaps you need to develop a supportive network. Once you, your family, and your friends accept your orientation, which can sometimes take a long time, you will feel better about yourself. Staying "in the closet" means hiding parts of yourself from those you care about. Even when this is done for a good reason, it can create stress.

If you choose to come out, select a time that *you* think is best and most appropriate for your family. Do not blurt out the revelation during an argument about something trivial (such as use of the family car) or at an inappropriate time (such as a holiday meal, when all the relatives have gathered around your family's dinner table).

Most parents of children who come out eventually accept their homosexuality. If your parents do reject you, try to help them accept the situation, but be aware that the process of acceptance can take a while, and even then you may not be successful.* Keep in mind that in the final analysis, it is your acceptance of yourself that really counts. What else can you do? See notes at the end of the chapter.

It is tragic that a significant number of gays and lesbians have attempted or have actually committed suicide because of guilt, fear, or societal pressure. Please read the following message I received from a teenager who wanted you to know his story.

You may be having suicidal feelings because you think you are gay. I know how you feel because I have had the

* Suggest they read one or more of the books listed near the end of this section on page 93.

same feelings. It is very frightening to think that some of our friends make jokes and comments that ridicule homosexuality.

You may feel that you don't want to tell anyone about your feelings. I know that I thought my friends and family would never understand. But keeping your fears bottled up will only make you feel more depressed and alone. The support of trusted friends will help you. Talk with someone you like and trust—your rabbi, a teacher, a relative, a friend. Make the choice based on who you feel will be the most supportive and understanding. You may also wish to find a psychologist or psychiatrist for professional counseling.

My closest friends and immediate family know now that I am gay and they have all assured me of their support. I only told them after I attempted to kill myself. I know now that I could have had their support all along and saved us all a great deal of anguish. So don't assume that others will "hate" you if you are gay. Give your friends a chance to be your friends.

If you notice suicidal feelings, ask yourself, Do I really believe that I deserve to die for having homosexual feelings? The question is almost too ridiculous to answer. Of course you don't!

You may be gay and you may not be. Many people have homosexual experiences and then go on to lead heterosexual lives. You will not know who you are until you overcome the fear and anxiety and allow yourself the time and space to explore your sexual orientation.

You may think that if you are gay you will suddenly be transformed into the stereotype of gay men: effeminate, talking with a lisp, meeting other guys in the men's room. Don't be taken in by crude stereotypes. It is quite possible to lead a full, successful, and happy life as a homosexual. There are people with stable and loving sex lives among both heterosexuals and homosexuals, and there are people with promiscuous sex lives among both heterosexuals and homosexuals.

It will be helpful to you to read novels, see films, or read nonfiction on homosexuality. This will make the topic of homosexuality less threatening and mysterious to you.

Your process of finding your sexual orientation *will* be difficult and at times painful. Don't make it more difficult by keeping all your worries to yourself and thus taking the risk of falling into a serious, or even suicidal, depression.

If you are troubled about homosexuality, find a sympathetic counselor with whom you can talk. Stay away from those who claim they can "cure" homosexuality and from people who are homophobic. One way to find a person with whom you can talk is through your local gay and lesbian hot line. Almost every major city has one. In New York, the telephone number of the Hetrick Martin Institute at 2 Astor Place, New York, NY 10002 is (212) 674-2400. The institute was founded some years ago to help confused or troubled gay, lesbian, and bisexual teens.

Anyone who is concerned about homosexuality should read *Disturbed Peace* by Brian R. McNaught (Dignity, 1981). Recommended books for parents whose child is homosexual (or who are worried about that possibility) include *Now That You Know: What Every Parent Should Know about Homosexuality* by B. Fairchild and N. Hayward (updated ed., Harcourt Brace, 1989), *Are You Still My Mother?* by Gloria Guss Back (Warner Books, 1985), *Bridges of Respect* by Katherine Whitlock (2d ed., American Friends Service Committee, 1989), *Twice Blessed—On Being Lesbian or Gay and Jewish* edited by Christie Balka and Andy Rose (Beacon Press, 1989), and Brian McNaught's *Now That I'm Out, What Do I Do?* (St. Martin's Press, 1997).

When you can't decide what to do, or when you receive negative responses from your parents, you can discuss your situation (anonymously) by contacting the Web site Outproud (**www.outproud.org**) or calling the hotline at 1-800-347-8336 (after 7 P.M. Central time). Also, most major cities have gay churches or synagogues. (For churches, look up Metropolitan Churches. Call your Union for Reform Judaism regional office for the name of a gay synagogue www.urj.org/offices.shtml).

You can also contact an organization called PFLAG (Parents, Families and Friends of Lesbians and Gays) at 1-202-467-8180. They will be very supportive.

Several of their pamphlets are extremely helpful, including:

- "Read This before Coming Out to Your Parents: A Guide for You and Your Parents"

- "Be Yourself: Questions and Answers for Gay, Lesbian and Bisexual People"

For more information, write to:

PFLAG (Parents, Families and Friends of
Lesbians and Gays)
1726 M Street NW, Suite 400
Washington, DC 20036
Web site: **www.pflag.org**

We might as well come to terms with the idea that one's sexual feelings can feel fixed, transitory, or change in time.

And if it is kept private, not flaunted or exploited, your sexuality is none of anybody's business (except if you want to discuss it with a friend, or a therapist or write a novel about it). Some people are secure in their feelings that they are heterosexual, homosexual, or bisexual (this means being open to both sexes). There are a small number of people who feel themselves to be transgendered (born into the wrong sex). This is not necessarily something to be concerned about unless it persists past puberty and you are unsure how to resolve your feelings about your gender identity. Help is available by calling one of the appropriate groups under the "Gay, Lesbian, Bisexual, and Transgender" section of the Resources list at the back of the book.

More on sexual orientation

Intersex is a wholly different category of sexual identity. Though it is quite a rare occurrence, some people are born with what is called an "intersex" sexual identity. That means that they are born with mixed sexual anatomy, in other words, with some degree of both male and female sexual characteristics. It's important to be clear that intersex is different than transgender. Some people who are transgendered were born intersex, but most were born with "standard" male or female anatomy.

Some people worry that they might be homosexual even though they never had a homosexual experience. Some people are abused and they think they have to become like the abuser or feel that their life is "over." If you've been victimized, you need to rise above it and not give any "credit" to the abuser. Some people like to dress like the opposite gender. Some people don't have any strong sexual feelings whatsoever. The only real issue is not to hurt yourself, hurt others, or be exploited because of your sexual feelings at any time.

Think you're pregnant? To be certain, you might begin with a home test. If your test is positive, see a doctor. Being pregnant is bad news if you don't want to be. But it's not the worst thing in the world. Talk to your parents. Most parents will help. If you feel you absolutely can't confide in your parents, then go to a Planned Parenthood Center or a family planning counselor. If you are opposed to abortion, go to a Birthright Clinic. It is your choice to have an abortion or complete the pregnancy. A good counselor will help you to make your decision without influencing you either way.

Pregnancy

The main thing is that you don't do anything to hurt yourself because of your pregnancy. Why punish yourself twice? If you've made an error in judgment, turn it into a lesson, not a tragedy. Learn more about birth control and risky sexual behavior, and then use the information to avoid making the same mistake again.

Why risk pregnancy in the first place? There are many problems related to teen pregnancy. Most of the dreams you had about the good life will be spoiled or rendered unlikely when you have to assume the responsibility of parenthood prematurely. Even an abortion may not be without medical or emotional risks.

So perhaps it is worth avoiding having sexual relations while you are a teenager. But if you decide to have sex anyway, always use birth control methods. Under no circumstance allow the male "in" without the use of a latex condom. Don't fall for the line, "I get no feelings when using a condom." That's his problem, not yours.

Special Note: For information on emergency contraception (what to do after unprotected sex), see the appendix entitled "Choice USA."

97

About 50 percent of females and 70 percent of males are likely to have sexual intercourse before they are 18.

Those who remain virgins are often maligned by their peers.

Virgin rights

I believe that virgins also have rights and that they ought to be respected for the courage to stand by their convictions.

Abstention should not mean ignorance about sexual issues. People who abstain from intercourse but are involved in intimate sexual relationships would do well to learn everything they can about the pleasure and pleasuring possible besides intercourse.

As a psychologist, I am frequently asked if it is normal to postpone sex until marriage. I reply yes but add, "If you are going to wait, I trust you won't expect fireworks on your wedding night. The decision to put off sex until marriage is a moral value and as such has nothing to do with fulfillment or pleasure."

Because human sexual pleasure and response are primarily learned activities, a person's first sexual experience should not be taken lightly. Obtaining responsible answers to the questions "When?" "Why?" and "With whom?" is important.

If I were to cite some of the most important characteristics of a good relationship or marriage, the list would include:

· Love, sensitivity, caring, trust, and respect

· A sense of humor

· Sex

· Sharing household tasks

98

Disappointment in love is often a cause of depression. Many people confuse sex with love. There are people who have exciting sex and don't even like each other, and there are others who love each other very much but have uninspired sex lives, at least in the early stages of the relationship. About the dumbest thing anyone can do is marry for sex or "chemistry," as it is often called. Even well-intentioned adults tell young people things like, "If you have sex before your wedding, you'll have nothing to look forward to in marriage. There'll be no surprises." I say that if sex is the only thing to look forward to in a marriage, don't marry. It's not worth it.

Some say that love is blind. I say that it's only blind for twenty-four hours. Then you have to open up your eyes and see the person you are in love with. Love at first sight? Maybe, but better take another look. The plain fact is, if you feel that you are in love, you are. But there arc two kinds of love—mature and immature. It's not difficult to tell the difference. Mature love is energizing. Immature love is exhausting. An immature relationship tends to leave you tired. You procrastinate a lot. You don't do your schoolwork or your job well. You avoid your domestic responsibilities. ("Me? Wash the dishes? I can't do that! I'm in love!") You have what is called a hostile-dependent relationship. You can't bear to be away from the person you think you are in love with. But when you are together, you fight and argue most of the time. Mood swings and accusations of jealousy, even violence, characterize the relationship. Some people even confuse love and hate because of the emotional "charge" that they feel. But if someone beats you up or forces sex upon you, that is not love.

How can you tell if you are really in love?

It's neurosis, dependency, or fear, but not love. In an immature relationship one person usually repeatedly asks, "Do you love me? Do you really love me?" I advise the other person to say, "No." You'll then have your first real conversation.

Immature relationships are characterized by promises like, "Don't worry, honey, when we get married, I'll stop fooling around with other women [men]." You might as well know now: A bad situation is *always* made worse by marriage.

Immature relationships reveal insensitivity and self-ishness by one or both partners.

Mature relationships are full of energy. You have time to do almost everything you want to do. You don't shirk responsibilities. When you are together, you enjoy each other. You might argue sometimes but not that much. You want to please each other.

How can you tell if what you feel is infatuation or mature love? In the first month you can't. (In the summer it takes two months.) Infatuation and mature love appear and feel exactly the same. But when the relationship settles in, all or some of the above-mentioned signs will appear, and you will be able to tell if you are *really* in love.

Here are some good general rules: Sex is never a test or proof of love. You can't buy love with sex. So many females, even in these enlightened times, have sex because it might lead to love, but many more males have sex because that is all that they want. A large number of males find it easier to make out than to make conversation. Some males are programmed by warped media messages to exploit females. Some immature males think that the number of times they have sex is a measure of their masculinity. When you get right down to it, friendship is the key to developing the relationship you want.

MATURE LOVE NURTURES.

IMMATURE LOVE CAUSES PAIN.

For more details, read *How Can You Tell if You're Really in Love* by Sol Gordon (Adams Media Corp., 2001).

Additional resources:

The Art of Loving by Erich Fromm (Perennial Classics, 2000)

Making Intimate Connections by Albert Ellis and Ted Crawford (Impact Publishers, 2000)

Love is a Verb by Bill O'Hanlan and Pat Hudson (W. W. Norton and Co., 1995)

Why Love is Not Enough by Sol Gordon (Adams Media Corp., 1990)

To Stand in Love by Paddy S. Welles (Geist and Russell, 2001)

Dying for love?

If you *truly* love anyone—your parents, your friends—you won't kill yourself. No matter how shabbily you feel that you have been treated by someone you care about, would you really want to bring such horrible pain to those whom you honestly love? They don't deserve it! You don't deserve it! If you feel desperate as a result of a fight or a breakup with someone you care about, don't act immediately. The emotions you are feeling will subside in time, and your view of what has happened will probably change dramatically. Give yourself and those you love a break. Sentencing yourself to death is not a rational move. Get help and talk the whole thing out with someone you trust. Don't take your life while you are in the middle of an emotional crisis. Your view of what has happened to you will change in time. Give yourself the gift of time.

When Scott Difiglia, a teenager from Plano, Texas, committed suicide because his girlfriend Kathy rejected him, he wrote a letter telling why he couldn't live with himself any longer. He concluded:

I am really sorry for letting everybody
down. Mom and Dad, I really love
you a lot
and I am really sorry. Thanks for putting
up with all my shit for so long.
All my love forever,
Scott

What Scott did had nothing to do with his love for Kathy or his parents, however sincere he felt about it.[*] Real love *always, always* means that a person cares more about the people he or she loves and their needs than about his or her own feelings.

We mourn for Scott, but we mourn for his family and Kathy even more.

[*] See the article about Scott in *Rolling Stone*, Nov. 8, 1984. (While this article was published a long time ago, Scott Difiglia's story remains a very tragic example of the consequences of misguided thinking.)

Chapter 4

Parent Concerns

It is possible that your parents don't understand you.

It is possible that you are more sensitive than your parents are.

It is possible that your parents don't care about you or are abusive.

But in most cases, parents do care, or at least one parent does. They do love you. But sometimes they don't know what's right for you or how to express it. Sometimes they are so preoccupied with their own troubles that they lose sight of yours. All parents have periods of time when they honestly don't understand their kids.

If a particular problem is not very serious, ask your parents to read the section titled "A message to parents." But before that read "A message to you: don't turn off your parents."

If you feel you can't talk with your parents of if you think they just don't understand you, it's still important for them to at least listen to you. You may need to do something special to get them to pay attention to you. Copy the messages below (or write you own) and leave them around where your parents can find them. Pick the time carefully. And then risk telling one or both your parents how you feel. Don't hold anything back. It's possible that it won't work. But at least you tried.

If you don't get along with your parents

Don't give up. There may be other opportunties to reach out to your parents. A school counselor or trusted aunt or uncle or other adult might be able to set up and mediate a meeting between you and your parents. But in the end you may have to manage without parental support. Sometimes you may have to count on a friend's parents for help. It's still possible to manage. Don't try to take revenge. Your parents may need your forgiveness. Remember what we've said before: The best "revenge" is living well.

If you don't have the parents you want now, when you become a father or mother, become the father or mother you would have liked to have had.

Dear Mom,
I'm in deep trouble.
I need to talk to you.
I want you to listen to me without
criticizing me.
It's important.

Dear Dad,
I'm in deep trouble.
I need to talk to you.
I want you to listen to me without
criticizing me.
It's important.

One of the most difficult concepts for many young people to accept is that their parents are good people.* Most parents mean well even if they seem old-fashioned and don't always make sense to their children. To you, parental restrictions may seem like hostility; to your parents, they represent concern for you.

Whether you like it or not, getting along with parents generally is an essential aspect of becoming a reasonably well-adjusted adult. In some cases, children may be better adjusted than their parents. Although it is still possible for those young people to manage in life, it takes a lot of courage.

So if you've had some stormy times with your parents lately, and especially if you feel they are not listening to you, here are a few suggestions that almost all parents would appreciate:

- Make it a point to spend a couple of hours a week with your parents.

- Every once in a while, ask a parent who works outside the home, "How are things going?" (If he or she answers "Fine," say, "I mean I'd like to hear more about your job/business.")

- Ask one or both parents for advice about something not too crucial so that you can easily follow their suggestions.

- Ask your folks about their lives when they were your age. You may gain some insights into why they feel the way they do about your activities, attitudes, etc. If they won't talk about their lives, you can be pretty sure it was painful. In any case, you will understand their approach to you better.

A message to you: don't turn off your parents

107

---

* Some parents, of course, are abusive. If your parents fall into this category, it's up to you to "rise above" them. The situation is not your fault, so don't punish yourself twice.

- Begin with telling the truth about aspects of your life that you have not been truthful about. If necessary, start by saying, "I worry that if I tell you the truth, you'll be very upset" or "When I tell the truth, the whole thing gets blown up out of proportion, so I am reluctant to be honest and open with you."

- Clean up your room at unexpected times.

- Take out the garbage or do the dishes without being asked.

- Compliment your parents on things that they do well.

- It's never okay to be rude to your parents.

Another way of improving your relationship with your parents is to embark on a one-month politeness campaign. Make it a point to be polite without sounding phony or sarcastic. This may require some practice in front of your mirror. Say things like, "Good morning," "Thank you," "Excuse me," and when you feel unusually generous, "I have a free hour. Is there a chore that you would like me to do?" Your mom or dad may ask if you are feeling well after that one! Or they might say, "What's gotten into you?" or "What took you so long to decide you're human?" Your response might be, "I haven't been very considerate lately. I'm trying to change to see if being considerate will make things more pleasant."

Let the experiment continue for at least a month, and then evaluate the results. If you have been working toward something you want, ask for it in this way: "I'd like to talk with you about something. Please hear me out, and then I would like to hear your thoughts on the subject." You may discover in the process that politeness makes life much easier for you, even if you don't get what you want. Although being polite is not always a sure method of getting closer to your parents, it can be a way of keeping your distance, which, in time, will give you the opportunity to discover your own way. You may then decide to close the gap or maintain a polite relationship, but that's up to you.

This approach may seem contrived, but it's still a good way to end a period of noncommunication and improve relations at home. All adults appreciate even a little effort. If you don't think this is so, try this method on an irksome teacher.

Did a divorce or separation, or living with a step-parent, mess you up?

Divorce or separation affects millions of children living at home and away at college. The situation for a large number of young people often improves as a consequence of divorce. Living with one loving parent is a relief after surviving years of living with two parents who are constantly fighting, arguing, perhaps abusing each other, and sometimes abusing the children as well. However, many young people from separated families have found themselves in really bad circumstances for various reasons. These children of separated or divorced parents:

· Feel deprived.

· Face economic hardship.

· Have many added responsibilities.

· Miss the absent parent.

· Are caught in the middle and are sometimes forced to take sides.

· Feel angry or abandoned.

· Are so worried about the divorce or separation that their schoolwork and friendships are affected.

· Feel guilty because they think the break up was their fault.

If any one of these things or related issues have affected you, here are some things that you can do and ideas that you can think about.

First and foremost you must recognize that if your parents break up, *it's not your fault*. You are not responsible even if a parent in an angry, impulsive moment blames you.

Life may be tough right now. Life may seem unfair. You

may feel depressed, but that's not a reason to punish yourself twice. It's unfortunate that you don't have the family life you want, but that's not a reason to fail in school, be rotten to the people you live with, or do things that are self-destructive (like taking drugs). You need to resolve and ensure that you won't make a bad situation worse by hurting yourself. *Now* is particularly the time to protect yourself, to be nice to yourself. Try at least to be polite to a parent or stepparent you don't like. Your attitude might change if you acquire more understanding or make an effort to forgive. You may want to consider counseling.

In any case, however far off it may seem, you will soon be working or in college. You'll be able to make your own decisions, live your own life, marry, and have children of your own. The *only* way you can achieve all this is by preparing yourself now. Get the grades you want and earn the money you need.

You may have to postpone some pleasures. You will have to avoid inadequate "solutions," like alcohol. You will need to practice patience and learn to tolerate frustration. But that does not mean your life has to be grim. You can still have relationships. Try to develop at least one intimate friendship. You need someone in whom you can confide. Develop an interest in at least one thing you can be passionate about. Be helpful to at least one person more vulnerable than you are. Make a commitment to at least one cause.

By reaching out beyond your own (perhaps even really bad) situation, you could be a source of comfort to others and, strange as it may seem, an inspiration for yourself. You will feel energized.

111

A message to parents

Parents:

No, you don't have to compromise your values.

No, you don't have to shift from being old-fashioned (which most parents are) to being what people call progressive, liberal, or "with-it."

Yes, you may have to improve your communication skills.

First you must recognize that adolescence is not a disease or a terrible stage that all young people go through. Many young people actually enjoy their adolescence.

Teenagers need to be appreciated and accepted as family decision makers. They should be in on problems, even serious ones, such as unemployment, fatal illnesses, and impending divorce. Teenagers feel rejected if they are excluded from family conferences. They need to have parents who are available to listen to their problems and take them seriously.

Never, never make fun of or mock a teenager's love affair. Young people's feelings are as strong as those of mature adults but are generally of shorter duration. It doesn't matter one bit if you are sure that the relationship won't last.

Please don't say things like, "You'll get over it," or "When you get older you'll laugh about this," or "It's just puppy love."

It's all right not to like your child's friends or choice of boyfriend or girlfriend. State your feelings, especially if a particular relationship seems to be having a bad effect on your child's attitude toward school or within the home environment.

You can simply state that in your opinion good relationships are "contagious." They make people feel good about themselves and are energizing. People in good relationships do well in school and can afford to be responsive to their parents.

But no matter how you feel, you should always be polite to your teenager and to his or her friends.

THE MOST IMPORTANT RULE IS:

NEVER, NEVER BREAK OFF COMMUNICATION

WITH YOUR CHILDREN,

NO MATTER WHAT THEY DO.

This does not mean that you can't express how you feel about a particular situation. Try not to have a standard response to all crises.

I asked my college students to recall a single sentence that most characterized what they considered inappropriate parental responses to a serious problem they had. A surprisingly large percentage of students, even those who claimed they got along reasonably well with their parents, recalled sentences like:

From mothers

· Life is tough all over.

· Count your blessings.

· Where did I go wrong?

· Go ask your father.

· Shut off the noise box.

113

From fathers

- Life isn't fair.
- Moderation, moderation.
- For crying out loud.
- Go ask your mother.
- Life is too short to be miserable.

If you want to have a serious talk with your child, please don't start with the following (which are guaranteed to turn off young people):

- When I was your age....
- It's about time you got good grades (*or* straightened your room).
- That's not your idea, is it?
- Wipe that smile off your face.
- After all we've done for you!
- What will the neighbors say?
- Are you telling me the truth?
- Act your age.
- As long as I don't know about it.
- Get off your high horse.

And please, don't ever tell a teenager not to worry. When was the last time someone told you not to worry and you stopped?

You may have teenagers who do a lot of things you disapprove of: They don't clean their rooms, they don't take their homework seriously, and they watch too much television.

Try to make a point of dealing with one thing at a time. Some parents tend to talk too much and complain about the whole spectrum of problems instead of concentrating on a specific issue or issues. Concentrate on only one or two issues and temporarily ignore everything else. This is usually a successful response only if you try at the same time to improve the quality of your relationship with your teenager by becoming involved in experiences together.

Telling teenagers all the "don'ts"—don't smoke, drink, get high, have sex, stay out late—doesn't accomplish much unless we can also help them discover positive ways to behave that will make them feel good about themselves.

Suppose the main problem is that your teenager chronically stays out late and does not come home at the prescribed time. On one particular occasion the teen had promised to be home on time but comes home an hour late without having telephoned. The parents are waiting up, furious that a promise has been broken and worried about the child's safety. As the teenager approaches the front door, he or she reviews his or her made-up explanation for being late (a broken-down car and a traffic jam are old favorites).

After having had a good time with friends, the teenager arrives home tense and anxious, anticipating the confrontation. The parents' own anxiety has built to the boiling point as a result of hours of fretting and the fact that the teen has been late practically every Saturday night for the past two months. During the fight that begins as soon as the door is opened, no constructive communication takes place. What the parents' anger is saying to the teenager is, "We don't trust you. You are a louse for making us so upset." Often the punishment administered is too severe for the offense. If grounding works, fine, but first evaluate the duration and effectiveness of the punishment and the possible dissension it can create.

The next time your teen is late say, "I'm very disappointed that you didn't keep your promise" and then leave the room. This is sure to generate guilt. Please realize that a prolonged shouting match will dissipate any guilt your teenager might feel.

There is nothing wrong with generating guilt in a teenager who has misbehaved. It's nonsensical to argue that all guilt is undesirable. Irrational guilt that overwhelms a person is not helpful, but rational guilt, which organizes a person and helps him or her avoid repetition of undesirable behavior, can be a constructive force—at least until the hoped-for "good judgment" kicks in.

At this point I would like to state my opposition to physical punishment under any circumstances. It tends to create even more anger and alienation and to intensify conflict. Few things turn kids off more than a slap across the face.

Sometimes parents forget that adolescents need models more than they need critics. They want their parents to respect their integrity and privacy and to include them in family matters. Above all, perhaps, they want love that they can return and information that can lead to self-acquired wisdom.

If your child shuts you out, knock gently on his or her door and say softy, "Honey, I love you. I really need to talk" or "Do you need a hug? I sure do!" or "I want to understand what just happened between us. Please help me."

Persist even if you are told to go away.

Don't wait for a crisis to tell your child that you love him or her. All of us, even the most independent teenagers, need hugs and kisses, or at least a friendly pat.

Be sure your teen knows that you are always going to help and support him or her. No matter how awful the crisis, you will not turn your back on your child. Rejection is not a part of a parent's role. You may not accept some behaviors, but the person is not the behavior. If your child thinks that you are always mis-understanding him or her or that your responses are somehow "off the wall," ask your child to tell you and then try to change your approach. If nothing else, this change might improve communication between you. The more respect you show your teen, the more respect you will get.

If you tell kids that they will never amount to anything or that they are stupid, they might believe you.

Don't give your children the impression that they have only one option. Try not to say things like, "If you don't go to college [don't pass math], you're doomed." It is better if you say, "It's my [our] hope that you will go to college [pass math with flying colors, or whatever]. If that is not going to happen, we need to discuss alternatives, and I think I can offer some help."

117

Above all, allow your children to express what they feel, whether it is unhappiness, disappointment, sadness, or joy. The feelings belong to them, and you don't have to share them, just accept them. Trying to understand a teenager can be hard work, especially when you remember how easy life was with this same person just a few years ago, but the rewards are worth it. I believe that the more sensitive we are to young people today, the more they are going to try to understand and be understanding in the future.

The main responsibilities of parents to their children are to:

- Love them.
- Talk openly with them.
- Nurture them.
- Help them turn their mistakes into lessons.
- Promote their self-confidence.

Parents who take these responsibilities seriously have a good chance of raising responsible adults who will feel affection and love for their parents.

Please note: The overwhelming majority of parents mean well and love their children, but nobody can be a perfect parent. When the uniqueness of each child, birth order, parental age (young or old), changing family circumstances, and a host of other variables are all taken into account, it is a tribute to human nature that any of us turns out to be "normal." Jerome Kagan, a noted psychologist, stresses in his book *The Nature of the Child* (Basic Books, 1994) that we have greatly overemphasized the role of parents as *the* determining factor in how children develop. Parents are important, of course, but so is the fact that children are born differently fearful, irritable, and alert. Their peers and the media also influence them.

The majority of mothers tend to blame themselves for whatever happens. They also tend to receive most of the praise if things work out well, even though today's fathers are much more involved in child-rearing. I recommend that parents read *Right from Wrong* by Michael Riera and Joseph Di Prisco (Perseus Publishing, 2002).

119

Don't operate on the assumption that, these days, young people know everything about sex. Where are they getting their knowledge—from parents, school, church, or synagogue? No, most of what young people "know," they get from one another, videos, films, magazines, or television, and most of it is just plain wrong.

"Askable" parents raise sexually responsible children

Parents could be the best sex educators for their own children. I believe that the public will applaud the *real* sexual revolution—when one's sexual behavior is private, moral, responsible, and pleasurable, and when people respect each other. It will come. The question is, what do parents do in the meantime? (Giving messages like "just say no" is useless).

Five critical things parents need to know:

1. Parents are the main sex educators of their own children, whether they like it or not.

2. Parents, if they want to be "askable," must be prepared for any question or incident that involves their children's sexuality. The best first response: "That's a good question."

3. Parents must convey to their children that nothing that ever happens to the child will be made worse by talking about it to the parent. The best first response: "I'm so glad that you are able to talk to me about this."

4. Children are not perfect, just as parents are not perfect. Young people make mistakes and it's up to parents to turn kids' mistakes into opportunities for learning and growth.

5. Failure is an event—it is never a person. Children

who are loved grow into adults who like themselves and others. They don't exploit others and are unlikely to let themselves be exploited.

What to do now? Current reality obligates parents to have frank and knowledgeable discussions about such issues as where babies come from, erections, wet dreams, menstruation, correct language for intimate body parts, the size of penis and breasts, and masturbation (it's *normal* and *private,* <u>not</u> bad). Young people need direct advice from their parents, such as, "If someone says to you, 'If you really love me, you'll have sex with me,' that is always a line to trick you and use you. If the person loved you, he/she wouldn't try to manipulate you that way."

Recommended publications and books

The Surgeon General's Call to Action to Promote Sexual Health and Responsible Sexual Behavior (2001) (David Satcher, M.D.) This publication is available on the Web at **www.surgeongeneral.gov/library**

Raising a Child Responsibly in a Sexually Permissive World by Sol and Judith Gordon. (Adams Media Corp., 2000)

Beyond the Big Talk: Every Parent's Guide to Raising Sexually Healthy Teens by Debra W. Haffner (Newmarket Press, 2001)

What's Up as You Grow Up? by Mary Jo Podgurski. Academy Press, 1997 (call toll-free 1-888-301-2311)

121

Growing Up Feeling Good: The Life Handbook for Kids by Ellen Rosenberg. Lima Bean Press, 630 Shore Rd., Suite 505, Long Beach, NY 11561

The Sex Lives of Teenagers by Lynn Ponton (reissue paperback ed., Plume, 2001)

Ask Me Anything by Marty Klein (Pacifica Press, 1996)

Love Undetectable: Notes on Friendship, Sex and Survival by Andrew Sullivan (Alfred A. Knopf, 1998)

From Diapers to Dating: A Parent's Guide to Sexually Healthy Children by Debra W. Haffner (Newmarket Press, 1999)

Raising Cain—Protecting the Emotional Life of Boys by Daniel J. Kindlon and Michael Thompson (Ballantine Books, 1999)

There's No Place Like Home... for Sex Education by Mary Gossart. Call Planned Parenthood: 541-344-1611, ext. 23

How to Talk with Teens about Love, Relationships and S-E-X: A Guide for Parents by Amy G. Miron and Charles D. Miron (Free Spirit, 2002)

For what the Jewish tradition says about sex: *Sex in the Texts* by Paul Yedwab (UAHC Press, 2002)

For a publication list of sexuality books for children, call Prometheus Books at 1-800-421-0351

Useful Web sites

SIECUS: **www.SIECUS.org**

Planned Parenthood Federation of America: **www.plannedparenthood.org**

Advocates for Youth: Suite 206, 1025 Vermont Ave. N.W. Washington, DC 20005 **www.advocatesforyouth.org**

For the *Religious Declaration on Sexual Morality, Justice and Healing* Contact the Web site of the Religious Institute at **www.religiousinstitute.org**

Also recommended: the three video series

Sex: A Topic for Conversation by Sol Gordon. Texas Media Projects, Inc. 5215 Homer Street, Dallas, TX 75206. 1-214-826-3863

Chapter 5

God Concerns

First you need to know that God can't do everything. We can't ask God to change the rules of nature for our benefit. I believe that God does, however, help those who stop hurting themselves.

Rabbi Harold S. Kushner expounded on these ideas in his wonderfully warm, deeply religious book titled *When Bad Things Happen to Good People* (Avon Books, 1983), which he wrote after experiencing a personal tragedy.

Rabbi Kushner says that God might not prevent calamity but God does give us the strength and the perseverance to overcome it.

Prayer cannot bring water to parched fields, nor mend a broken bridge, nor rebuild a ruined city; but prayer can water an arid soul, mend a broken heart, and rebuild a weakened will.

—*Gates of Prayer* (Central Conference of American Rabbis, 1975), p. 152

Are you disappointed in God?

Rejecting religion is understandable if you expect faith to alter natural events but discover that it does not, or if you believe that God will allow only good things to happen to you but you are instead experiencing many problems. Only you can give yourself a good life.

Have you lost faith in religion?

It is, however, appropriate to agonize over why your religion hasn't helped you feel better about yourself. Discuss the issue with your rabbi, priest, or minister. You might get some surprising answers.

Having a meaningful religious identity can help you feel better about yourself and others.

Here is what I think.

There is a way for everyone

People who want to mock God
say there is only
one road to heaven.
God knows
a one-way sign is a
dead end,
leading to nowhere,
God knows
there are infinite ways to find
your own way.

John Donne, a Roman Catholic priest, theologian, and philosopher, suggests that we give up the search for certainty and go on a voyage of discovery and understanding. He feels that the question to ask is not "Is there a God?" but rather "What is God?"

When heavy burdens oppress us and our spirits grow faint and the gloom of failure settles upon us, help us to see through the darkness to the light beyond.

To You, O God, we turn for light; turn to us and help us.

When we come to doubt the value of life because suffering blinds us to life's goodness, give us the understanding to bear pain without despair.

To You, O God, we turn for understanding; turn to us and help us.

When we are tempted to suppress the voice of conscience, to call evil good and good evil, turn our hearts to the rights of others and make us more responsive to their needs.

To You, O God, we turn for guidance; turn to us and help us.

And when we become immersed in material cares and worldly pleasures, forgetting You, may we find that all things bear witness to You, O God, and let them lead us back into Your presence.

To You, O God, we turn for meaning; turn to us and help us.

—*Gates of Prayer* (Central Conference of American Rabbis, 1975), p. 392

Spirit is not in the *I*, but between *I* and *Thou*. It is not like the blood that circulates in you, but like the air in which you breathe. Man lives in the spirit, if he is able to respond to his *Thou*. He is able to, if he enters into relation with his whole being. Only in virtue of his power to enter into relation is he able to live in the spirit.

—Martin Buber, *I and Thou* (Scribner, 1978)

Do you feel in need of prayer?

127

Chapter 6

What Is the Purpose of Life?

Does life have a purpose?

Martin Buber, reflecting on the philosophy of the Baal Shem Tov, the great Chasidic master, suggested that every person born into this world represents something new, something that never existed before.

All of us have the task of actualizing our unprecedented and never-recurring potentiality and not the repetition of something that another has already achieved. Everyone is unique because had there ever been anyone like you, there would be no need for you in the world.*

I was blown away when I read the Baal Shem Tov's powerful statement of purpose for each of us. It immediately reinforced my belief that not only was I unique and special, I also had a mission. And while I could never be fully certain what that mission's exact nature was, I *knew* that I was on the right track when the following words came to me.

Everybody
is
unique.
Compare not
yourself
to anybody else,
lest
you spoil
God's curriculum.

* Read *The Way of Man According to the Teaching of Hasidism* by Martin Buber (The Citadel Press, 1950).

My becoming a writer didn't depend on anyone else's agreeing that I should be one. If you are on the right path, one person is a majority.

Viktor E. Frankl has explored in depth the meaning of life in his remarkable book *Man's Search for Meaning* (rev. ed., Touchstone, 1984). Frankl, a psychiatrist and Holocaust survivor, argues that the meaning of life is always changing. One can discover its varying meanings in three different ways:

· By turning suffering into an achievement.

· By deriving from guilt the ability to change oneself for the better.

· By finding an incentive for action. There is never a good reason to be *stuck* in any kind of suffering. The potential for change is always present.

Here is Frankl's advice to all of us:

Don't aim at success. The more you aim at it and make it a target, the more you are going to miss it. For success, like happiness, cannot be pursued. It must ensue, and it only does so as the unintended side effect of one's personal dedication to a cause greater than oneself or as the by-product of one's surrender to a person other than oneself.

Frankl sees "surrender" as the giving of ourselves to a loving relationship.

IT'S NOT GIVING UP, IT'S GIVING TO!
IN THE GIVING, YOU SHALL RECEIVE!

If someone asks you what is happening in your life, could you give a response that approximates one of the following answers?

- I'm in love.

- I'm an artist.

- I'm working for world peace.

- I'm into my schoolwork.

- I'm a big brother/sister to a little kid I care about.

- I've joined the Audubon Society.

- I work as a volunteer at the Children's Hospital.

Without a sense of purpose, life doesn't seem very exciting or meaningful. That's why so many people end up filling the emptiness of their lives with despair, addiction to TV, sex, violence, drugs and alcohol, and passivity.

How does forgiveness work?

Here is the voice of a Holocaust survivor, Rabbi Arthur Schneier:

I can say that if anything, I have been strengthened as a result of the Holocaust. Instead of just taking my energy and being bitter and resentful, I was able to harness this energy for positive bridge building with people of other faiths, with people of other ideological persuasions. That is the price I must pay for my survival.

Rage is destructive and renders survival meaningless. Forgiveness frees you to be your own person. It is energizing. It offers you another opportunity to be optimistic. You become a hero. Give it a try.

Start by forgiving your parents, a friend, or someone you love who has rejected or betrayed you. Often these people mean well, even if they hurt you. Don't they say, "I'm doing this for your own good"? But sometimes they know not what they are doing.

Hate is exhausting.

Forgiveness makes love possible again.

Just because you feel unloved now doesn't mean that you are unlovable.

I do not believe that we must forgive everyone for every act. You may not want to forgive the rapist, the mugger, the people responsible for the Holocaust. However, for your own mental health if nothing else, you should forgive the people who have hurt you but did so without malicious or conscious intent, as well as those who realize their mistakes and ask your forgiveness.

As for those you cannot forgive—the rapist, the mugger, the murderer—why give them the ultimate victory by punishing yourself for years? Sure you'll be hurt and upset and might need help to recover. But recover fully you must. You must shout out, "I'm alive! I'll protect myself. Enough of suffering. I'll help others. I'm determined that this terrible event will not destroy my life. I will live well!"

A young friend of mine who made three suicide attempts before he was twenty-one objected to my emphasis on forgiveness. He is now thirty-five, very much alive, vibrant, creative, and thrilled that he didn't kill himself. He wrote:

As I explored my spiritual being, I have suc-ceeded in overcoming self-hatred by working with unconditional love, unconditional acceptance, and compas-sion. These concepts keep me spiritually equal to others and do not presume— which forgiveness does—that I'm better than anyone else.

He views compassion, not forgiveness, as the key. I'm not sure. But it's something to think about.

If you can't forgive someone who hurt you or if you can't accept the idea of forgiveness

It's never too late

It's never too late

- To try again
- To grow again
- To share again
- To risk again
- To feel again
- To change again
- To love again
- To be enthusiastic again
- To read *Winnie the Pooh* for the first time

There are no rules for mourning. There are no stages you must go through. My friend Marion Leavitt says, "Every death has a life of its own."

I have been comforted by the following meditation. Perhaps you will be, too.

It is hard to sing of oneness when our world is not complete, when those who once brought wholeness to our life have gone, and naught but memory can fill the emptiness their passing leaves behind.

But memory can tell us only what we were in company with those we loved; it cannot help us find what each of us, alone, must now become. Yet no one is really alone; those who live no more echo still within our thoughts and words, and what they did is part of what we have become.

We do best homage to our dead when we live our lives most fully, even in the shadow of our loss. For each of our lives is worth the life of the whole world; in each one is the breath of the Ultimate One. In affirming the One, we affirm the worth of each one whose life, now ended, brought us close to the Source of life, in whose unity no one is alone and every life finds purpose.

—from *Gates of Prayer* (Central Conference of American Rabbis, 1975), p. 625

When someone you love has died

How is hope renewed?

Hope is renewed

- When we talk about our feelings.
- When we confide in someone.
- When we realize that we can influence our own lives.
- When we develop relationships.
- When we realize that all moods are temporary.
- When we do mitzvot.
- When we practice forgiveness.

How can you tell when hope is being renewed? You'll feel energized and optimistic. You'll realize that the people who care about you are not complete without you!

Ideas to Push You Into Thinking About Your Life

Chapter 7

Sometimes it takes
the death of someone close,
an awareness,
"There go I
by the grace of God"
(I could have been gassed in the Holocaust),
a recovery from a terrible illness or accident,
surviving a catastrophe
or a "simple" mugging

to discover how marvelous it is
just to be alive
with all our imperfections.

Some people are lucky.
They know this without
being reminded by tragedies.

I've been reading *The Road Less Traveled* by M. Scott Peck (Simon & Schuster, 1978). Peck sees life as a series of problems that require resolution. He says that the difference between mature and immature people depends on successful and unsuccessful resolution of problems. He puts a heavy emphasis on discipline, and he helps us appreciate that the process of confronting and solving problems—a lifelong process—is painful. For him the whole process of meeting and solving problems is what makes life meaningful. Problems call forth our courage and wisdom. Carl Jung suggested, "Neurosis is always a substitute for legitimate suffering."

137

My friend Gloria Blum says, "There are no mistakes, only lessons."

How does one find peace in a dreadful world? I struggle with conflicting thoughts. They are not harmonious, and they don't all make sense. It's a matter of struggling with priorities, finding out what's important, what your particular mission in life is. All too often, we go on with our daily lives, of course, occupied with unimportant things. We don't spend time thinking about the things that are worth thinking about. The Talmud says, "Just as the hand held before the eye can hide the tallest mountain, so the routine of everyday life can keep us from seeing the vast radiance and the secret wonders that fill the world." The philosopher William James wrote, "Wisdom is learning what to overlook."

We each have a responsibility to find out what meaning life has for us, knowing full well that this is a lifelong process. How can we put to use our uniqueness to develop ourselves and in the process be useful and helpful to others? Many people today are depressed mainly because they feel useless.

Surely we have to do our daily tasks, even though many of them are boring. The most meaningful and joyous experiences in life are of brief duration. But what are we to do in the meantime?

I think we have to do more mitzvot.

I think we need to reduce our fear of vulnerability by exposing ourselves to uncertainty by taking risks.

A stunning book titled *Number Our Days* by Barbara Meyerhoff (Simon & Schuster, 1980) includes the following passage, in which someone describes a dream:

"A man of great wisdom, a doctor told me I had a fatal disease. 'You cannot remedy it,' he said. 'There is nothing I can do for you except to give you this advice: Do your work as well as you can. Love those around you. Know what you are doing. Go home and live fully. The fatal disease is life.'"

"This is very interesting," Shmuel said. "The Jews do not have much of an idea about afterlife. Everything is how you live here. You should be good to others. You should pay attention to your history. You should always be wide-awake so you can be responsible for what you do. God wants more of the Jews than to survive. The Jews must choose to be alive. So for once, I would have to say you had a very Jewish dream."

I live my life almost fully and with energy, but I have some regrets, personal distresses, and genuine disappointments. Suffering is personal and cannot easily be shared.

My survival depends upon
a sense of humor
a sense of purpose
a sense of mission
a sense of meaning
a sense of beauty
a sense of nonsense
a common sense
a passion for *bittersweet*
    plays
    ballet
    movies
    music
    art
    novels
    chocolate and
    intimacy

June 12 is my birthday. Send bittersweet greetings.

139

New journeys, experiences, and people call forth a *new you*. Why eighteen? In Hebrew the word *chai* means "life," and its numerical value is eighteen. *Chai* is my favorite number.

1. *The existential question* is how you come to terms with life, not death.

Eighteen slogans and thoughts

2. You cannot find yourself through

   · drugs

   · dieting

   · complaining

   · getting laid

   · watching TV

   · movies

   · eating

   · jogging

   · making a fast buck

   · violence
   or in

   · bars

   · cults

   · parties

   Only through relationships based on mutual respect can you find yourself.

3. Ridicule is making fun of other people's pain.

4. People who feel good about themselves (most of the time) do not allow themselves to be exploited, nor do they want to exploit others.

5. Not everything in life can be understood or resolved. All of us have some areas of vulnerability. Sometimes the best we can do isn't good enough.

Some of us live in places where the winters are cold and long. That's why it's good to be optimistic.

6. Really marvelous experiences occur infrequently, do not last long, and are rarely scheduled.

7. "It is characteristic of wisdom not to do desperate things." (Henry David Thoreau)

8. Food can make you feel full, but fulfillment comes only with love.

9. If you have a tendency to put yourself down, struggle against it. It's boring to be with people who are down on themselves.

10. "Each individual is a unique being beyond the reach of diagnostic categories, an artist overflowing with the will and freedom to shape his or her own fate." (Otto Rank)

11. Nobody can make me feel inferior without my consent.

12. Intimacy is joyous and sad. It is sharing and open-ended, and it takes your mind off yourself momentarily.

13. "In order to perfect oneself, one must renew oneself day by day." (A Hasidic saying)

14. Love is where it's at and that's a fact. (A refrain from a not-yet-composed popular song)

15. "All the way to Heaven is Heaven." (Saint Catherine)

16. "Honesty is not necessarily self-disclosure. It is saying only what you mean." (Sylvia Hacker)

17. Suffering may not enhance your life, but recovery will.

18. Vibrations are real.

Thoughts and things to do for the next eighteen days

Day one: Letting go of the ghosts of the past will permit you to have the life you're ready for today.

Day two: Let go of any thoughts that don't enhance your life.

Day three: Give someone the benefit of the doubt.

Day four: You don't have to prove yourself to anyone today.

Day five: Say no when you mean no. This frees you to mean yes when you say yes.

Day six: Offer a friend some of your energy.

Day seven: If you've wronged someone, ask that person to forgive you.

Day eight: Today say only what you mean.

Day nine: There is nothing you need to do first in order to be enlightened.

Day ten: Share a dream with someone.

Day eleven: Grow by coming to the end of something and by beginning something else.

Day twelve: Set yourself a simple task and complete it today.

Day thirteen: Express your appreciation to someone.

Day fourteen: Realize that maturity is the capacity to endure uncertainty.

Day fifteen: Teach someone something new.

Day sixteen: Turn one of your mistakes into a lesson.

Day seventeen: Expect a miracle but don't count on one.

Day eighteen: Seek peace first within yourself and then share it.

Everybody is unique and has a particular mission in life. One of the old Hebrew Sages is reported to have said on his deathbed, "God will not ask me why I was not like Moses. He will ask me why I wasn't myself."

If you haven't reached the point of loving and caring for yourself, the best way to change is to do mitzvot—be helpful to others (especially underprivileged and abused people). When you begin to feel respected, needed, wanted, and appreciated by others, you'll be amazed how you'll begin to feel love for yourself and have the capacity to love others.

Think about it!

Are you making the following mistakes?

1. Comparing yourself unfavorably with others. There will always be people who appear to be better looking, richer, luckier, and better educated. We are all created equal in the eyes of God. We are all created different to serve God in a special way.

2. Feeling that you won't amount to much unless

   • Someone falls for you.

   • Someone envies you.

   • Someone needs you.

   • You earn a lot of money.

   • Your parents are satisfied with your achievements.

3. Thinking you must please everyone. You must first please yourself and thereafter only those people you care about. People who try to please everyone end up pleasing no one.

143

4. Setting unreasonable goals for yourself. Lower your standards to improve your performance. You can always advance beyond today if you want to.

5. Looking for *the* meaning of life. Life is not a meaning. It is an opportunity.

6. Forgetting that life is made up of meaningful experiences that are mainly of short duration but repeatable.

7. Deciding that your fate is determined by forces outside of yourself. Maybe it is, but you can usually control your attitude about the difficult or good circumstances of your life. More often than not, it is attitude that makes the difference.

People who feel good about themselves

- Are enthusiastic.
- Have a sense of humor.
- Have interests.
- Enjoy being helpful.
- Are unselfish.
- Don't exploit others.
- Do not allow themselves to be exploited.
- Don't make fun of others.
- Have a sense of their own special mission.
- Can begin again.
- Turn their mistakes into lessons.
- Are optimistic.

- Are willing to take risks.

- Know how to listen.

- Encourage others to feel good about themselves.

How can you feel good about yourself? Recognize that you are unique. Stop comparing yourself with other people. Believe that you can stand on your own merits.

When or if you have children, raise them to like themselves. That's the most important thing. Don't criticize them for things that they can't change. Don't force them to excel in areas in which they have no interest or talent. Praise their uniqueness in small ways every day. Children who like themselves develop into adults who like themselves.

It's not enough to have lived. We should be determined to live for something.
May I suggest that it be creating joy for others, sharing what we have for the betterment of personkind, bringing hope to the lost and love to the lonely.

—Leo F. Buscaglia

Jonathan's Song

By Owen Dodson (1914-1983)*

(For Sol Gordon)

I am part of this:
four million starving
And six million dead:

* A poet—and a friend—who wrote about the Holocaust.

145

I am flesh and bone of this.

I have starved
In the secret alleys of my heart
And died in my soul
Like Ahab at the white whale's mouth.

The twisted cross desire
For final annihilation
Of my race of sufferers:
I am Abel, too.

Because my flesh is whole
Do not think it signifies life.
I am the husk, believe me.
The rest is dead, remember.

I am a part of this
Memorial to suffering
Militant strength:
I am a Jew.
Jew is not a race
Any longer—but a condition
All the desert flowers have thorns,
I am bleeding in the sand.

Take me for your own David:
My father was not cruel,
I will sing your psalms,
I have learned them by heart.
I have loved you as a child,
We pledged in blood together.
The union is not strange,
My brother and my lover.

There was a great scent of death
In the garden where I was born.

Now it is certain:
Love me while you can.

The wedding is powerful as battle,
Singular, dread, passionate, loud,
Ahab screaming and the screaming whale
And the destination among thorns

Love is a triple desire:
Flesh, freedom, hope:
No wanton thing is allowed.
I will sing thy psalms, all thy psalms,
Take me while you can.

How to Save Your Own Life

by Erica Jong

1. Renounce useless guilt.

2. Don't make a cult of suffering.

3. Live in the now (or at least in the soon).

4. Always do the things you fear the most. Courage is an acquired taste like caviar.

5. Trust all joy.

6. If the evil eye fixes you in its gaze, look elsewhere.

7. Get ready to be eighty-seven.

(to be continued)

"The best thing you can do for yourself is to forgive yourself. There'll be plenty of sunuvabitches to beat on you and say ugly things. Guilt is a loser's game. You can't get back yesterday, or even this afternoon."

—Harry Crews, *A Childhood: The Biography of a Place* (reprint ed., University of Georgia Press, 1995)

Crews adds, "The only way to deal with the real world was to challenge it with one of your own making."

Here are some thoughts that I had as I was putting the final touches on this book.

- Everybody makes mistakes. Turn mistakes into lessons.

- You are not alone. It only seems that way sometimes. Many people have the same feelings that you have.

- It's not your feelings that get you in trouble. It's your method of escape.

- We need to learn to accept our limitations and our emotional frailties.

- Why be ordinary if you can be extraordinary?

- Accept criticism only from people you respect.

- Why travel heavy if you can travel light?

- Someone is going to have a good day today. It might as well be you.

Chapter 8

A Special Message for School Counselors and Youth Leaders

Why "at-risk" youth do not pay attention to what we (so-called) educators have to say

Despite all the gloom and doom about today's youth, the majority—let us say more than two-thirds—grow up to be relatively healthy, law-abiding, mature, drug free adults.

But the problem of "at-risk" youth, for whom we pay a huge price in crime, suicide, health issues, and severe psychological problems, exists. While poverty, prejudice, and the images prevalent in the media are factors in at-risk status, in my judgment there are more crucial reasons that damage young people.

At-risk youth are those who generally have not learned to read. (More than half the people in prisons today are virtually illiterate.) They are prone to violence, bullying, sexual promiscuity, homophobia, and are already on the road to becoming alcoholics and/or drug addicts. They may be on huge ego trips and could be excessively overweight.

The reason most "just say no" programs are not

working is that we spend our energy addressing symptoms without significantly remediating the one component common to each of our troubled youngsters: low self-esteem. We talk about it, but few educators understand how to help children feel good about themselves. Remedial reading is a good example. We take children who hate to read for five minutes and remediate them with a reading program for an hour or more! Haven't we gotten the message yet? You can't unblock a block with a block! Don't we understand that at-risk children equate education with submission? Their most debilitating characteristic, a need for instant impulse gratification, surfaces as they seek to be in control. They self-medicate their "depression" with drugs, sex, and/or violence.

All dangerous behaviors must be addressed fully and realistically, but our overriding concern needs to be the promotion of self-esteem. Children and teens who know they count and feel they are cared for do not engage in antisocial behaviors. *Caution:* Don't fall for the trap of equating self-esteem with "feeling good about yourself." Felling good about yourself can sometimes be an excuse for selfish, greedy, and uncaring behavior. It is surprising how many people feel good about themselves while being nasty to those around them. (Not understanding this fact is the main reason why self-esteem has gotten a bad reputation in recent times.)

When you have positive feelings about yourself, you have energy, you are optimistic, and you treat the people around you with kindness. You can afford to be generous because your world looks hopeful.

I like the definition of self-esteem developed by the California Legislative Task Force on Self-Esteem (1990): "Appreciating my own worth and importance and having the character to be accountable for myself and to act responsibly toward others." Self-esteem is most related to this concept: *I am* because *I can.* Without a sense of genuine achievement, self-esteem is mockery.

Promoting self-esteem among the so-called children at risk presents a challenge to be creative and to *know* those children. Teach each one something new—postpone remediation and allow time for the individual child to accomplish something worthwhile. Then, teach reading. Secondly, encourage at-risk children to do good deeds, be helpful to others. It's a biblical injunction to do mitzvot. You don't have to start out by feeling good about yourself in order to be helpful to others. The process of doing good eventually creates the atmosphere of high esteem. No amount of anti-sex, -drugs, -suicide education will help much without a person feeling useful, needed, and accomplished. To be more precise—just telling young people not to smoke, drink, or bully has virtually no impact on youth who suffer from low self-esteem.

Start out by telling young people, "If you already have a bad habit (drinking, smoking, etc.) it is very difficult to stop." Then you can explain that virtually all at-risk behavior is related to the need to reduce or alleviate

153

distress or tension in your life. Until you do that, the chances of *stopping* are minimal. Then explore the issues in the child's life that are leading to low self-esteem.

Have we not noticed that the children who are "functional" have passionate involvements, are optimistic about the future, have realistic goals, have hobbies, and have relatively good relationships with their parents?

Explore the needs of at-risk youth. What's missing in their lives? A mentor, a hobby, after-school programs, physical exercise, transfer to job corps for older youth? Perhaps psychological counseling. However, parents should be very hesitant about antidepression or attention-deficit medication for their children. Virtually none of these drugs has been carefully researched over a long period of time. Without monitoring on a regular basis, they should not be used.

Can't we see how ludicrous it is to eliminate gym classes, music, and after-school programs? The "Leave No Child Behind" program has contributed virtually nothing to improve the educational system, especially not the training of teachers. And what about the virtual elimination of sex education programs in schools? The introduction of abstinence-only courses will have almost no impact on the sexual health of young people today. It may even be harmful, especially for boys and girls with low self-esteem. While teen pregnancy has been reduced somewhat (not because of abstinence, I dare say, but because of increased condom use), the sexually transmitted disease rate is skyrocketing, especially among young people who think that oral sex is not sex.

What about children who have been abused or otherwise traumatized? I encourage youth who have been victimized to take revenge. But what I carefully explain is that the best "revenge" is living well. It's a sane and effective approach to victimization. For example, I counseled a 17-year-old who had been physically abused repeatedly by his father. (The father said he did it because he loved him.) Did he forgive his father? No. Not, at least, until and unless his father begged or pleaded for forgiveness. When he has children of his own, he should never hit them. Never. Loving them as he had wanted to be loved would be his revenge. The worst thing that happens in so many cases is that the victim identifies with the aggressor and becomes like him. Victims should focus on doing good and not assume that what happened to them was in any way their fault.

The person who was raped might be encouraged to volunteer in a rape crisis center or join a women's group that is occupied with this issue. Youth who have been traumatized could serve as mentors to abused or neglected children. This would be revenge. It doesn't help to act as though life is over or to distrust others in the future based on past traumas. What can one do to change his or her thinking?

- Remind oneself that one should not remain victimized by traumatic and agonizing experiences of the past.

- Remain hopeful about the possibilities of change.

- Allow revenge to enable one to let go of feelings of unworthiness.

155

Focus on being helpful to others. Do mitzvot.

I agree with Lauren Slater, who suggests in an article in *The New York Times Magazine* of February 23, 2003, that some traumatized people may be better off "repressing" the experience rather than illuminating it in therapy. For some people, going over and over the same incidents makes them worse. If this appears to be happening, consider terminating treatment and focus more on the present. Do good deeds, learn something new, and develop good friends.

Something we all need to ponder—Martin Buber expressed it the best in his book *The Way of Man*. He wrote:

Every person born into this world represents something new, something that never existed before, something original and unique. "It is the duty of every person . . . to know and consider that he is unique in the world in his particular character and that there has never been anyone like him in the world, for if there had been someone like him, there would have been no need for him to be in the world. Every single man is a new thing in the world, and is called upon to fulfill his particularity in this world . . . ." Every man's foremost task is the actualization of his unique, unprecedented and never-recurring potentialities, and not the repetition of something that another, and be it even the greatest, has already achieved.

This is certainly a message that needs promotion at home and in the schools.

Let me conclude by telling you the story of my life (slightly abbreviated).

Growing up as an idealistic youth, I was determined to save the world—the more I tried, the world became worse and worse. Then I decided I had taken on too much. I thought I would just try to save the United States. The more I tried—conditions in the United States got worse and worse. So again I thought I had taken on too much. So I decided I would just try to save my neighborhood. My neighbors told me to mind my own business. But just as I was about to give up in despair, I read in the Talmud that if you can save one life, it's as though you have saved the world. That's now my mission—one person at a time.

Choice USA: Leadership for a Pro-Choice Future

Emergency Contraception

- Emergency contraception (or EC) is just that—contraception. It prevents pregnancy before it starts.

- Emergency contraception is ordinary birth control pills taken after unprotected sex in high doses to prevent pregnancy.

- EC pills are taken in two doses—the first dose must be taken within seventy-two hours after unprotected sex and the second dose is taken twelve hours later.

- In most states, you must have a doctor's prescription to obtain EC from a pharmacy—this prescription will either be for the correct type and amount of birth control pills or for the pre-packaged EC pills such as Preven or Plan B.

- Emergency contraception is very safe; according to the FDA serious complications almost never occur.

- EC works before implantation and will not

The difference between Emergency Contraception and Mifepristone (RU-486)

159

terminate an already established pregnancy. If a woman is pregnant when she takes EC, there is no effect on the fetus or the woman.

- For information on where to obtain emergency contraception from a Planned Parenthood clinic you can call **1-800-230-PLAN.** For a list of other EC providers call the Emergency Contraception Hotline at **1-888-NOT-2-LATE** or visit their Web site at **www.not-2-late.com.**

Mifepristone

- Mifepristone (RU-486) is a pill that is used to terminate early pregnancies.

- Mifepristone blocks the action of progesterone, a hormone that sustains pregnancy. As a result, changes occur in the woman's uterine lining, causing the embryo to detach.

- Mifepristone must be used within forty-nine days of a woman's last menstrual period.

- Mifepristone, prescribed as Mifeprex, must be obtained from a doctor and requires three visits to the doctor.

- Mifepristone must be taken in combination with another drug called misoprostal, which is administered during the second required doctor's office visit.

- Research has shown that complications associated with mifepristone are very rare. Over 500,000 women in Europe and the United States have used mifepristone safely and effectively over the past decade.

- Mifepristone does not replace the need for access to surgical abortion. Some women may prefer a surgical abortion, may not know they need an abortion until after 7 weeks into the pregnancy, or may have health conditions that make them unable to use mifepristone.

- Visit **www.earlyoptions.org** for information on mifepristone. To find an abortion provider in your area call the National Abortion Federation Hotline at **1-800-772-9100.**

Resources

General Information on Substance Abuse and Other Addictions

National Institute on Drug Abuse
www.health.org
1-800-662 HELP
Confidential information and discussion for all ages, referral services for those seeking treatment.

National Council on Alcoholism and Drug Dependence
www.ncaad.org
1-800-NCA-CALL
Open twenty-four hours a day to send information and refer calls to local NCA affiliates for counseling and treatment referral.

Parents' Resource Institute for Drug Education (PRIDE)
www.prideyouth.com
1-800-241-7946
Information, free materials, and referral to local parent groups.

National Drug Abuse Treatment Referral and Information Service
www.drughelp.org
1-800-COCAINE
Information, counsel, and referral to treatment centers.

Partnership for a Drug-Free America
www.drugfreeamerica.org
1-212-922-1560
Communications materials and campaigns designed to change public attitudes about drugs, making them less attractive.

Mothers Against Drunk Driving
www.madd.org
1-800-GET-MADD
Develops public awareness programs at local, state, and national levels to stop drunk driving and support victims.

American Lung Association
www.lungusa.org
1-212-318-7000
Fights lung diseases with special emphasis on asthma, tobacco control, and environmental health.

International Centre for Youth Gambling Problems and Other High-Risk Behaviors
www.education.mgill.ca/gambling
800gambler.org

Responsible Gambling Council
www.cfcg.org

National Inhalant Prevention Coalition
www.inhalants.org
1-800-269-4237
Explains the dangers of inhalants, develops prevention campaigns, and answers questions.

Inhalant Abuse: Join Together's Hot Issues
**www.jointogether.org/sa/issues/hot_issues/
inhalants**

Teachers. The Anti-Drug
**www.theantidrug.com/get_involved/
learninhalants.html**

TCADA: Inhalants
www.tcada.state.tx.us/research/inhalants

Center for Internet Studies
www.virtual-addiction.com
1-800-504-7000 ext. 14
Resource for information on cyber living, internet,
and computer addiction.

Campaign for Tobacco-Free Kids
www.tobaccofreekids.org

Canadian National Clearinghouse on Tobacco
and Health
www.ncth.ca

PrevLine
www.health.org

Tobacco Bulletin Board Service
www.tobacco.org

Addiction Support Groups

Alcoholics Anonymous World Services
www.alcoholics-anonymous.org
1-212-870-3400
International fellowship of individuals with drinking
problems.

Gamblers Anonymous
www.gamblersanonymous.org
1-213-386-8789
Provides a fellowship for compulsive gamblers to
deal with and overcome their addiction.

Overeaters Anonymous, Inc.
www.overeatersanonymous.org
1-505-891-2664
Overeaters Anonymous is a fellowship of individuals who, through shared experience, strength, and hope, are recovering from compulsive overeating.

Eating Addictions Anonymous
**www.dcreregistry.com/users/eating
addictions/index.html**
1-202-882-6528
A twelve-step recovery program for men and women recovering from all forms of eating and body-image addiction.

Workaholics Anonymous
www.people.ne.mediaone.net/wa2
1-510-273-9253
A twelve-step program to curb this addiction.

Debtors Anonymous
www.debtorsanonymous.org
1-781-453-2743
A fellowship of men and women who share their experience, strength, and hope with each other that they may solve their common problem and help others to recover from compulsive debting.

Marijuana Anonymous
www.marijuana-anonymous.org
1-800-766-6779
Dedicated to the recovery of marijuana addiction.

Narcotics Anonymous
www.na.org
1-818-773-9999
Narcotics Anonymous is an international,

community-based association of recovering drug addicts.

Nicotine Anonymous
www.nicotine-anonymous.org
Nicotine Anonymous is a fellowship of men and women helping each other to live lives free of nicotine.

Sex and Love Addicts Anonymous
www.slaafws.org
1-781-255-8825
Sex and Love Addicts Anonymous is a twelve-step, tradition-oriented fellowship based on the model pioneered by Alcoholics Anonymous.

Sexaholics Anonymous
www.sa.org
1-615-331-6230
Sexaholics Anonymous is a fellowship of men and women who share their experience, strength, and hope with each other that they may solve their common problem and help others to recover.

Support Groups for Family Members of Addicts

Gam-Anon
www.gam-anon.org
1-718-352-1671
For spouses, family members, and friends of compulsive gamblers.

Al-Anon Family Group Headquarters, Inc. and Alateen
www.al-anon.alateen.org
1-888-4AL-ANON
To help families and friends of alcoholics recover from the effects of living with the problem drinking

167

of a relative or friend. Alateen is the recovery program for young people. Alateen groups are sponsored by Al-Anon members.

Co-Anon Family Groups, Inc.
www.co-anon.org
1-770-928-5122 Atlanta, Georgia
1-714-647-6698 Orange County, California
1-818-377-4317 Los Angeles, California
1-520-513-5028 Tucson, Arizona
A fellowship of men and women who are husbands, wives, parents, relatives, or close friends of someone who is chemically dependent.

Families Anonymous, Inc.
www.familiesanonymous.org
1-800-736-9805
A twelve-step, self-help, recovery and support-group fellowship for relatives and friends concerned about a loved one's problems with alcohol, drugs, or behavioral problems.

Nar-Anon Family Groups Headquarters, Inc. and Nar-Ateen
www.naranon.com
1-310-547-5800
Nar-Anon is a family support group for people dealing with the addictions of family and friends.

S-Anon International Family Groups, Inc.
www.sanon.org
1-615-833-3152
S-Anon is a fellowship of people who share their experience, strength, and hope with each other so

that they may solve their common problem of
sexaholism in a relative or friend and help
others to recover.

Domestic Violence and Child Abuse

Domestic Violence Anonymous
www.baylaw.org
1-415-681-4850
A program for women and men, who through shared
experience, strength, hope, and honesty, are
recovering from domestic violence.

National Clearinghouse of Child Abuse and Neglect
Information
www.calib.com/nccanch
1-703-385-7565

National Domestic Violence Hotline
www.ndvh.org
1-800-799-SAFE (7233)

Bulimia/Anorexia

American Anorexia Bulimia Associates, Inc.
www.aabainc.org
1-212-575-6200
Information for those with eating disorders and for
their friends and family.

Self-Injury

Focus Adolescent Services:
Self-Injury and Self-Mutilation
www.focusas.com/Selfinjury.html

Gay, Lesbian, Bisexual, and Transgender Youth Support Services

Outproud
www.outproud.org
Information for gay, lesbian, bisexual, and
transgender youth.

Youth Resource
www.youthresource.org
Information and peer support for gay, lesbian,
bisexual, and transgender youth.

Ambiente Joven
www.ambientejoven.org
Providing information and community for Latino gay,
lesbian, bisexual, transgender, and questioning
youth.

Healthy Gay, Lesbian, and Bisexual Student Project
www.apa.org/ed/hlgb.html

We Are Your Children Too: Accessible Child Welfare
Services for Lesbian, Gay, and Bisexual Youth
www.casmt.on.ca

General Teen Support Services

Teen Advice Online (TAO)
www.teenadvice.org
Information on teen problems through a worldwide
network of peers thirteen years of age and older.

Teen Scene
www.advocatesforyouth.org/corner.html
Information from the Advocates for Youth Web site.

Information on Teen Sexuality, for Parents

Campaign for Our Children
www.cfoc.org
Information for both parents and teens on talking
about sexuality.

National Parent Information Center
www.npin.org
Research-based information on parenting and family
involvement in education.

Sex Ed Mom
**www.thriveonline.oxygen.com/sex/experts/
sex_ed_mom/index.html**
Advice, live monthly chats, teaching tips, and video
clips for parents.
Talking with Kids about Tough Issues
www.talkingwithkids.org
Encouragement for parents to talk with their children
early and often about sexuality issues.

171

Planned Parenthood Federation of America
**www.plannedparenthood.org/library/
SEXUALITYEDUCATION/DEFAULT.HTML**
Information on "How to Be A Good Parent," "How to Talk with Your Child about Sexuality," "How to Talk with Your Teen About the Facts of Life," and "Human Sexuality: What Children Should Know."

The Planned Parenthood of Greater Northern New Jersey also has a number of age-appropriate books and videos about sexuality education, and can be reached at 973-539-9580, x120.

Information on Teen Sexuality, for Teens

Birds and Bees
www.birdsandbees.org
Information on birth control, pregnancy, STDs, and links to other sites.

Coalition for Positive Sexuality
www.positive.org
Information for teens who are sexually active or who are thinking about becoming sexually active.

Go Ask Alice!
www.goaskalice.columbia.edu
Question and answer site including information on relationships, sexuality, and sexual health.

gURL
www.gurl.com
Infromation on issues that affect the lives of girls thirteen years of age and older.

It's Your (Sex) Life
www.itsyoursexlife.com
Information for older teenagers about pregnancy,
contraception, and STDs.

Iwannaknow
www.iwannaknow.org
A safe and fun place for teenagers to learn about
sexual health and for parents to receive guidance.

Scarleteen
www.scarleteen.com
Advice, articles, and information addressing sexuality and sexual health issues for children and parents.

Sex, etc.
www.sxetc.org
Information, advice, and resources by teens for
teens (and parents, too).

Sex Sense
www.ppsp.org/tpe.html
Advice and quizzes for and by teens.

Sextalk
www.sextalk.org
Information on safer sex, self exams, and sexual orientation.

SIECUS
www.siecus.org
Starting place for teens to learn about sexuality
issues.

Teenwire
www.teenwire.com
Sexuality and sexual health information for teens.

173

Information on Sexually Transmitted Diseases

CDC National AIDS Clearinghouse
www.cdc.gov/nchstp
1-800-458-5231

American Social Health Organization
www.ashastd.org
P. O. Box 13827
Research Triangle Park, NC 27709
Phone: 1-919-361-8400
Fax: 1-919-361-8425
This organization is dedicated to stopping STDs and their harmful consequences for individuals, families, and communities.

National STD/AIDS Hotline
Phone: 1-800-342-AIDS (English)
1-800-344-7432 (Spanish)
1-800-243-7889 (TTY)

CDC National Prevention Information Network (NPIN)
info@cdcnpin.org
P. O. Box 6003
Rockville, MD 20849
Phone: 1-800-458-5231
Fax: 1-888-282-7681
This is the U.S. reference, referral, and distribution service for information on HIV/AIDS, STDs, and tuberculosis (TB).

National Herpes Hotline (NHH)
1-919-361-8488
This hotline provides information and referrals to anyone concerned about herpes. Trained Health

Communication Specialists are available to address questions related to transmission, prevention, and treatment of herpes simplex virus (HSV). The NHH also provides support for emotional issues surrounding herpes, such as self-esteem and partner communication. The hotline is open 9 AM to 7 PM, Eastern Time, Monday through Friday.

Organizations Involved in Suicide Prevention

Suicide Anonymous
1037 Cresthaven
Memphis, TN 38119
The only qualification for membership is a desire to stop living out a pattern of suicidal ideation and behavior.

NOPCAS
National Organization for People of Color Against Suicide, Inc.
P. O. Box 125
San Marcos, TX 78667

American Foundation for Suicide Prevention
www.afsp.org
120 Wall Street
22nd Floor
New York, NY 10005
1-212-363-3500
Works to increase awareness of suicide and

solutions that help survivors cope with their loss.

SPANUSA
Suicide Prevention Advocacy Network
www.spanusa.org
5034 Odens Way
Marietta, GA 30058

American Academy of Child and Adolescent
Psychiatry
www.ascap.org

Columbia University Teen Screen Program
www.teenscreen.org
1051 Riverside Drive
NYSPI Unit 78
New York, NY 10032
1-212-543-5016 or
1-212-543-5948

Link-Counseling Center's National Resource Center
for Suicide Prevention and Aftercare
348 Mt. Vernon Highway, N.E.
Atlanta, GA 30328
1-404-256-2919

The National Parent Consortium
www.natlparentconsortium.org
1130 17th Street, N.W.
Suite 400
Washington, D.C. 20036
1-877-463-6360

Pallotta Teamworks
2709 Media Center Drive
Los Angeles, CA 90099-8100
Raises funds for the American Foundation for
Suicide Prevention.

Compassionate Friends
www.compassionatefriends.org
P. O. Box 3696
Oak Brook, IL 60522
1-877-969-0010
An international support organization for families
who have experienced the death of a child.

American Association of Suicidology
4201 Connecticut Avenue, N.W.
Suite 408
Washington, D.C. 20008
1-202-237-2280

SAVE—Suicide Awareness Voices of Education
www.SAVE.org
7317 Cahill Road
Suite 207
Minneapolis, MN 55439-2080
1-952-946-7998

Nationally Recognized Local Suicide Prevention Organizations

Youth Suicide Prevention Program
yspp@mindspring.com
18511 15th Avenue, N.E.
Seattle, WA 98115
1-206-297-5922
Request "What Every Teacher Should Know About
Preventing Youth Suicide" as well as their
publication list.

177

Suicide Prevention Alliance
167 Moore Road
King, NC 27021
1-336-985-3136

Dide Hirsch Suicide Prevention Center (Los Angeles)
1-310-391-1253

Smile
P. O. Box 30357
Spokane, WA 99223-3005
1-509-448-8886
Request Smile Lines, a newsletter for friends of students mastering important lifeskills education.

Books on Suicide

The Clinical Science of Suicide Prevention, Herbert Hendin and J. John Mann, editors. Annals of the New York Academy of Sciences, vol. 932. Available from the New York Academy of Sciences; 2 E. 63rd Street; New York, NY 10021.

Counseling Suicidal People: A Therapy of Hope by Paul G. Quinnett. Available from the QPR Institute, Inc.; P.O. Box 2867; Spokane, WA 99220. Telephone (toll-free): 1-888-726-7926.

Help Me, I'm Sad: Recognizing, Treating, and Preventing Childhood and Adolescent Depression by David G. Fassler and Lynne S. Dumas (Penguin Books, 1998).

Lonely, Sad, and Angry: A Parent's Guide to Depression in Children and Adolescents by Barbara D. Ingersoll and Sam Goldstein (Doubleday, 1995).

Why Suicide? by Eric Marcus (HarperCollins, 1996).

Adolescent Suicide by Alan L. Berman and David A. Jobes (reissue ed., American Psychological Association, 1996).

Leaving Early: Youth Suicide, the Horror, the Heartbreak, the Hope by Bronwyn Donaghy (Harper Collins, 1997).

Recovering from Depression: A Workbook for Teens by Mary Ellen Copeland and Stuart Copans (rev. ed., Paul H. Brookes, 2002).

Journal of Suicide and Life Threatening Behavior The official journal of the American Association of Suicidology.

179